BINGE-EATING

A Beginner Comprehensive Guide to Permanently Ending Overeating, Maintain Mindful Eating and Weight Loss Therapy

Catherine Kowal

© Copyright 2020 - All rights reserved.

The content contained within this book may not be reproduced, duplicated or transmitted without direct written permission from the author or the publisher.

Under no circumstances will any blame or legal responsibility be held against the publisher, or author, for any damages, reparation, or monetary loss due to the information contained within this book, either directly or indirectly.

Legal Notice:

This book is copyright protected. It is only for personal use. You cannot amend, distribute, sell, use, quote or paraphrase any part, or the content within this book, without the consent of the author or publisher.

Disclaimer Notice:

Please note the information contained within this document is for educational and entertainment purposes only. All effort has been executed to present accurate, up to date, reliable, complete information. No warranties of any kind are declared or implied. Readers acknowledge that the author is not engaging in the rendering of legal, financial, medical or professional advice. The content within this book has been derived from various sources. Please consult a licensed professional before attempting any techniques outlined in this book.

By reading this document, the reader agrees that under no circumstances is the author responsible for any losses, direct or indirect, that are incurred as a result of the use of information contained within this document, including, but not limited to, errors, omissions, or inaccuracies.

Table of Contents

Introduction 1

PART ONE 5

Chapter 1: Understanding Binge-Eating 6

   Hunger Versus Appetite and Craving. 9

   Differences between Emotional and Physical Hunger 12

Chapter 2: When Eating Becomes An Emotional Addiction ... 13

   The Binge Cycle 16

   The Role of Hormones 18

   The Lies A Binge-Eater Tells Himself 19

Chapter 3: The Root Cause Of Emotional Eating 21

   Underlying Factors 22

   Risk Factors for Binge-Eating 24

   Precipitating Factors 26

Chapter 4: Do You Binge-Eat? 29

   Behavioral Signs 30

   Emotional Signs That You Are Binge Eating 34

   Diagnosis of BED 36

Chapter 5: Why You Should Not Binge-Eat 38

Chapter 6: How Binge-Eating Leads To Weight Gain 45
    Spike and dump syndrome 50
    Why you should be wary of gaining excess weight 53

PART TWO: DEFEATING BINGE EATING 61

Chapter 7: Weight Loss Therapy 62
    What To Eat 62
    What Should Drink 68
    How To Eat And Drink The Right Way 73

Chapter 8: Sugar Addiction And Binge Eating 80

Chapter 9: The Scourge That Is Processed Foods 89

Chapter 10: Cognitive Behavioral Therapy 97
    Cognitive Behavioral Therapy in Treating BED 103
    Scientific Assessment of the Efficacy of CBT
    for the Treatment of BED 108

Chapter 11: Other Therapies For Binge Eating Disorder 111
    Dialectical Behavior Therapy (DBT) 111
    Family-Based Treatment (Fbt) For Children And Adolescents 119
    Motivation To Change Therapy 120

Chapter 12: Essential Tips For Curing Binge-Eating 122
    Exercise as a palliative measure 122
    Medications 123
    How to Manage a Binge Eater 126
    Prevention of a Relapse 128
    Vital Tips for Curing Binge Eating 131

Conclusion 133

Introduction

Food is life, and that is no exaggeration. Our bodies as living things require external nourishment in the form of food to keep functioning optimally. We derive the essential elements that our body needs from food. So important is eating that it was Ancient man's only preoccupation. However, even eating has certain etiquette and rules that one must adhere to if it is not to supply some worries along with the essential nutrients it provides. We eat and feed our body with the nutrients from food. However, there is a safe limit for food consumption, beyond which we get discomforted and uncomfortable. There is only so much food that our bellies and bodies are designed to receive and hold at a specific period. Despite that, each one of us has been guilty of overeating in the recent past.

From time to time, everyone eats more food than they really should; an extra slice of pizza, a whole helping of ice cream, the fresh doughnuts at the picnic. We all indulge in overeating once in a while; that is not a problem. However, when eating goes beyond a desire to nourish and becomes almost an obsession that you need to satisfy regardless of whether you are full or not, there is a problem.

When you wolf down thrice the quantity of food you should eat in a day at a single sitting, the biology of your body takes a beating.

Do you overeat almost all the time? Do you find yourself wishing to eat even when you are not hungry? Do you often eat extra helpings, especially when you are alone? Do you find it hard to stop eating until your plate is empty? Do you eat on impulse rather than to satisfy real hunger? If any of the questions above seem to be talking to you, then you may already be a binge-eater. Luckily, you have a book that teaches you how to deal with binge-eating in your hand. I have written this book for all and sundry, especially the people who have lost control over their food choices. Because this is what binge-eating is; a loss of control over when, what and how to eat.

Eating is a biological process that offers us nourishment and satisfaction. It should not be a response to emotions or cravings. It should always remain under our control at all times. Sadly, binge-eaters get to lose this control. They do not eat to satisfy hunger; they eat in response to emotional triggers. This act causes a whole world of new issues when kept up for extended periods.

Now, as recently as a decade ago, binge-eating was not recognized as an evident eating disorder, but since its recognition, it has been acclaimed as the most common eating disorder in the whole planet. Since then, researches have continued to examine the intricacies involved in losing control over our eating pattern. This book delves into the most authoritative of these findings to bring you a lasting solution to binge-eating.

Binge-eating is not easy to deal with; many people who try to quit often experience relapses if not outright failures. However, I have structured this book in such a way that we flow from understanding what binge-eating is, to its signs, and lastly ways to overcome it.

However, this book is only useful if you give the tips within a trial, and stick to healthy eating habits. Good luck!!!

PART ONE

The goal of part one is to introduce you to binge-eating, its triggers and potential dangers it can cause. Just as importantly, you will also get to understand how binge-eating grows to be very hard to get rid of.

Chapter 1

UNDERSTANDING BINGE-EATING

What is Binge-eating? I could offer you yet another dictionary definition, but the world's veritable army of lexicographers have done justice to that. Instead, let me illustrate better with a short story.

James is overweight and has been trying to remain on a ketogenic diet for the last three months with varying degrees of success. Some days, he can stick to his diet plans. On other days, James succumbs to the craving to wolf down more than what he recognizes as healthy for him. Only last Friday, he had a very stressful day at work and got home late at night, tired. He took a shower, eat dinner, and laid on his bed. At the precise moment he laid down, he felt the urge to stick something into his mouth yet again. He knew he had had his fill at dinner and shouldn't go pile up more calories. Two minutes later, James stood in front of his opened fridge, ice cream bowl in hand and wolfed down the entire lot in less than two minutes. Then he closed his fridge and went back to bed. Immediately the door of his fridge closed; he became awash with guilt and shame at not being able to keep to his diet plan. He felt terrible with himself and swore never to allow the same to happen again. Deep down inside him though, he already knew he would get to devour the second bowl the next morning.

The story above aptly covers the cardinal points of binge-eating. James did not eat because he was hungry or even particularly because he liked ice-cream. Instead, he ate partly because he had wired his body system to demand excess food in response to his thoughts, and somewhat because he was stressed. That, in essence, is what binge-eating is; eating as a response to emotional impulses.

Binge-eating occurs when an individual consumes a large quantity of food rapidly in response to specific emotional triggers rather than genuine hunger. Simply overeating is not enough to qualify you as a binge-eater though; everyone overeats once in a while. Instead, the way you eat is only an indication of a much deeper problem in the interaction between you and food. Binge-eating is a physical, biochemical, and psychological disorder all at once. A binge-eater typically gets attracted to food when he is on a binge. This seemingly uncontrollable physical attraction leads to a change in the biochemistry of the body and leaves a psychological deficit to be made up.

Binge-eating itself though occurs most commonly as a part of two eating disorders; Binge Eating Disorder (B.E.D) and bulimia nervosa. Our discussion in this book shall revolve majorly about these two terms. What is BED, and bulimia nervosa? The American Psychiatrist Association defines BED; as

> *"... (series) episodes of binge-eating in which the person consumes large quantities of food in a very short time, often in secrecy from other people. "*

That means (frequent episodes of binge-eating characterize BED.) Bulimia Nervosa shares the same core principles with BED except that people suffering from Bulimia Nervosa get so distraught after bingeing that they attempt to purge the food they have just eaten out of their system. They may try to do this via a variety of ways. Some sufferers engage in marathon fasts, hoping to get rid of the food they have eaten or as atonement for binge-eating. Others may choose to induce vomiting to get rid of the food they just ate, or engage laxatives and diuretics to rid themselves of the wet weight of the food they consumed. It is even possible for chronic sufferers to participate in a strenuous, overboard exercise in the belief that it burns off the excess food they have eaten. Unfortunately, these all cause more damage than help.

They may choose excessive fasting, vomiting, laxatives, diuretics, or excessive exercise to get rid of the food they have consumed. We can consider Bulimia Nervosa a form of BED with the added attempt to get rid of the food that one consumes. Since you understand this already, I may use the term "binge-eating" interchangeably in this text. Just bear in mind that BED is differentiated from Bulimia Nervosa by attempts to purge.

Now, just how common is binge-eating? The stats speak for themselves. 3.5% of Adult American women and 2% of American men suffer from binge eating disorder while this figure may be as high as 16% in adolescents. Again, two-thirds of people with BED are overweight and actively trying to reduce their weight. That shows that BED is a real threat when it comes to nutrition in the 21st century.

Unfortunately, many people fail to understand that binge-eating can be a psychological disorder. Many people have embarked on weight-loss crusades lasting several months and even years, without any noticeable difference, all thanks to the fact that they binge-eat a lot. It is relatively common to find an individual who claims that he loves food a lot and can eat a mountain even when he is not hungry. Such a person might have "BED" without knowing it. As we will discuss later, binge-eating may even be the root cause of some of the social and health problems you are battling. Also, Binge-eating isn't just about the quantity of food that an individual consumes at a sitting, it is about how it gets eaten too; secretive, too rapid and too frequently. All these contribute to providing the ill-effects of binge-eating.

Hunger Versus Appetite and Craving.

What is the role of hunger and appetite in BED? Do they play any at all? Yes, they do! BED might as well be defined as a disorder characterized by a dysfunctional hunger-signaling system. Before then, what is the difference between hunger and appetite?

Hunger is a body signal to inform us that we are running low on food reserves and need to refill. When the body requires food supplementation for its activities, we get signs that tell us that the energy reserves are down. You may experience rumbling sounds in your stomach commonly known as hunger pangs; if not satisfied in time, hunger can lead to other signs such as weakness, fatigue, dizziness and a sensitive disposition towards people and tasks.

Appetite, on the other hand, represents our desire to eat to satisfy hunger. It is a measure of our interest in eating a particular food. It represents an impulse from the brain, directing us to start eating at a certain level or rate. Now, appetite is tightly regulated, so it doesn't get out of hand. Appetite may decrease or increase depending on the specific conditions you are in at that point. Your desire for a particular meal or food may increase, for instance, if you have not eaten it for some time, or you are quite hungry at that point. It may also decrease as fit, such as when an individual is ill or has just eaten. It is responsible for why sometimes you may feel hungry but have no desire to consume any of the food choices at hand.

Craving is a specialized form of appetite when you have the desire to eat a particular food item. For instance, we all get cravings every day. You may look at apples in a fridge and feel like eating one. That is a craving. Even thinking of a particular food can trigger the desire to consume that food as well.

Now, how do these three concepts affect binge eating? Let us take a look. When our body needs food, we get hungry. The appetite for food then satisfies our hunger. Therefore, if anything happens to disturb the balance created by these two forces, there is a chance that an abnormal eating pattern may arise.

In people with BED, for instance, they have lost control over their appetite, and it never seems to get satisfied even when they are full. So, they may continue to pile on food even when they are full. This is brought about by certain hormones as we shall discuss in the next chapter. The same thing applies to cravings. When a particular craving becomes unbelievably strong and demands to be satisfied frequently, it may lead you to eat more than is normal, consistently.

Any issue that arises with hunger too can lead to BED. We eat based on our appetite; therefore, it is essential to eat food only when we are hungry. Otherwise, there might be a problem if eating is allowed to continue in the absence of real hunger. For the basis of binge-eating, there are two primary forms of hunger: physical and emotional.

Physical hunger is real hunger characterized by growing pangs in the stomach and feelings of fatigue. This hunger is genuine, and everyone should try to respond to by eating. Eating gets rid of this form of hunger at once. Emotional hunger, on the other hand, is the scourge of binge-eaters. Emotional hunger is not real and is in response to your emotional state. Eating food does not solve it. Therefore, it is vital to be able to differentiate between these two types of hunger and eat only in response to real biological hunger.

Differences between Emotional and Physical Hunger

Physical Hunger	*Emotional Hunger*
Goes away after eating	Does not get fixed by eating
Physical signs of hunger such as dizzying	Most signs are in the form of thoughts, ideas, and opinions
The onset is gradual	It comes up suddenly.
Physical hunger can wait until the right time to eat.	It often demands instant satisfaction.
The craving is for a combination of a wide variety of choices	The desire is usually for comfort and luxury foods such as soda and chips for instance
Doesn't trigger negative emotions such as guilt and pity	Triggers feelings bordering on low esteem and guilt

Now that we have differentiated between the two forms of hunger, which one do you indulge in more frequently when you eat?

In conclusion, binge-eating as a form of emotional eating, causes people to eat in response to their emotional state and cravings (emotional hunger), rather than as a response to the natural state of hunger. Repeated episodes of binge-eating soon cement a state of permanence in one's eating pattern and can cause a whole bevy of health issue and social dysfunctions.

Chapter 2

WHEN EATING BECOMES AN EMOTIONAL ADDICTION

From the word "go," survival has always been our primary goal as a species, and the first step in securing survival has always been food. Food is the most-enduring, single component of human existence since the Big-Bang. Aside from nourishing our bodies, eating provides us with the chance to savor the taste of food and derive a primal satisfaction from it. A plate of food almost always changes our mood and lifts expectation and the atmosphere of social interaction.

Pleasurable at the highest level is the act of eating; so, it is a bit understandable that all humans grow to develop a fondness for the very act of eating besides it being a necessary biological act. However, even the greatest of pleasures must be kept under control. So, what happens when an individual loses control of the ability to regulate the joys that come with eating; chaos in the form of food addiction. Did I hear you snicker?

Yes, it is common to use the word "addiction" to refer to several unhealthy habits or obsession with a harmful substance. I inform you today that even food, that most dependable of external factors that we survive on, can be a source of addiction for you. How does this happen? How can you get addicted to food?

When we tamper with our perspective on what food truly is and turn it into an answer to our emotional states, then we grow addicted to it. You will not grow addicted to food because you like the taste of chips or you like feeling your stomach full. No, you will get addicted to food because it is your answer to every emotional state. Are you stressed? You pop a can of soda to calm your nerves. Anxious? You put a bar of chocolate in your mouth. Are you feeling tired and confused? You down two large plates of pasta and go to bed. Happy? You buy yourself a bowl of ice-cream. In need of energy and motivation? You get yourself an espresso at the nearest Starbucks. With time, food soon becomes the only response you know to every state of mind you are in at all times.

As the American Psychiatric Association puts it, "Addiction is characterized by an inability to consistently abstain, impairment in behavioral control, craving, diminished recognition of significant problems with one's behaviors and interpersonal relationships, and a dysfunctional emotional response."

Now, let's go through this widely accepted definition of addiction, and you can judge if as a binge-eater, you are addicted to food or not. Let's start with abstinence and control; a binge-eater cannot stop eating such large quantities because he has lost control. Even when you know your stomach is already full, you continue to pump the morsels into your system. Nothing shows an absence of self-control better. The definition also recognizes that cravings must exist for an addiction to be confirmed.

As a former binge-eater, I got irrepressible cravings for certain foods, and I just knew right away that I had to fulfill them. It didn't even matter where I was; immediately I got the cravings and impulses to eat a particular food, it became the most crucial point on my mind. Binge-eating also causes a lot of social problems as we will discuss later and affects the way you relate with others. The last point, ("dysfunctional emotional responses") is perhaps the clincher if you still have any doubts. Immediately after a binge, the typical binge-eater feels so guilty and a little angry with himself/herself. He is sorry for having eaten beyond his normal limits. However, this guilt does not stop him from satisfying his cravings the next time they hit him. Even as he stands guilty, a binge-eater is already planning his next binge deep in his subconscious mind. How more dysfunctional can an act get? How more can a person get addicted?

As if that was not enough, a full food addiction comes with the whole army of relapses, remissions, and withdrawals. That brings us to what I like to call "the binge cycle."

The Binge Cycle

As with every addiction, there is a cycle or sequence of repeated events that make it hard for an addict to quit his habit. The same thing applies to binge-eating. Binge-eating involves four sequential stages represented below.

- Tension buildup
- Bingeing
- Post Bingeing
- Resolution

i. Tension buildup

This stage is the first in any binge. It is where the initial impulse to eat arises. You may be working at something or feeling the effect of some negative emotions, and the suggestion pops in your mind that maybe you need a swig of Coke to get back to normal. Once the impulse gets planted in your head, it is tough to get rid of it. For most binge-eaters, this is also the stage where they plan for the next binge. They may even decide on what to buy and eat, whether to hide and hoard the items and when to binge. This is the trigger stage where you feel helpless to resist the coming binge.

ii. Bingeing

In this phase, you have been unsuccessful in fighting off the urge to eat. You have already decided to binge, and you are about to binge. The food you intend to binge upon is available and in more-than-sufficient quantity. Now, as you settle down to your business of overeating, there is always that little voice at the voice of your mind telling you this is wrong as you know full well that you do not need what you are eating to satisfy real hunger. The consequences of what you are doing run through your mind but you do not even notice. Your whole focus is on getting that ham and cheeseburger down into your stomach. Even when you begin to feel full, you do not stop until you have gorged yourself beyond reasonable limits. This actual phase of bingeing takes very little time to accomplish, usually occurring in less than five minutes.

iii. Post Bingeing

This stage is more mental than physical. It is the stage where you finally seem to have time for the little voice that warned you against bingeing. As you lay in discomfort brought about by excess food, you begin to reminisce about the ill-effects of what you have just done. The guilt becomes overwhelming, and you feel crushed and disappointed in yourself. Low self-esteem kicks in and at that point, you think less-worthy of your actual value. You may get disgusted and depressed at what you have done, and you wish you could undo it. It is also in this stage that people with Bulimia Nervosa try to purge or rid the body of the excess food they have taken.

iv. Resolution

This phase while common, does not always occur after every binge. Driven by discomfort, and feelings of guilt, binge-eaters try to make resolutions preventing bingeing from happening again. It almost always fails, of course. Chronic offenders or people already on a program to get rid of binge-eating are usually more touched; they may go even farther to get rid of some of the triggers or fast food items they have at home. All these doesn't stop them from bingeing the next time in most cases.

These four stages of binge-eating continuously repeat themselves in a cycle. First, the impulses arrive. You feel the need to eat a lot. Next, you make plans and get to eat beyond your control. Disgust and guilt sets in, you feel less of a human being and make plans that almost always fail to get off the binge-eating wagon.

The Role of Hormones

Hormones play a large part in determining if you are more likely to suffer from BED or not. Primarily, we have two hormones that control hunger; Leptin and Ghrelin. Leptin produced in the adipose tissue is known as the "hunger hormone." It is the hormone responsible for the pangs of hunger we get when the body needs food. After eating, the levels of leptin reduce telling the body that we are no longer hungry. Unfortunately, new research has shown that people with BED generally have higher levels of leptin. What this means, in essence, is that even when they eat, the leptin level does not drop by much. That means the brain is still getting signals that there is hunger after they have eaten.

The other hormone, Ghrelin, is the hormone of satiety. It communicates with the brain to tell it that you are full. Being deficient of sufficient levels means that one will not reach satiety. Such an individual may binge more regularly.

The Lies A Binge-Eater Tells Himself

With that in mind, how do binge-eaters manage to convince themselves to go on another binge despite feeling awful about the last episode? It is easy, really. Remember the little voice I mentioned in the second stage of the binge cycle. I know I made this voice sound like the good guy, trying to tell you not to eat more than is necessary, but it isn't. Instead, it occupies a dual, good-bad guy role. This same voice spends every other stage of the cycle criticizing your lifestyle choices. It is the same inner critic that makes binge-eaters feel bad and terrible about themselves. This same voice then turns around to help them convince themselves to binge. Therefore, in the periods leading up to a binge or during bingeing, binge-eaters often find lies or unconvincing facts to back their need to overeat.

I have gathered some of the more common lies that binge-eaters tell themselves here;

- I will take just a little bit and stop

- I need to eat this particular item, or I will be very uncomfortable

- …but I love eating a lot, and it makes me feel great

- I can always hide my binges from public consumption

- This food is to celebrate so-and-so

- It's been long since I last ate heavily

- Overeating cannot kill me

- I will exercise after this to atone for the excess food I am about to eat.

- I don't binge-eat all the time

- This is the last time ever

- I need to be stronger to kill this urge

- Work and family are great, who cares about what I eat?

- Bingeing just this once will not add ten kilograms to my weight anyway

With these kinds of rationalizations, a binge-eater will always find a way to justify his binges. It is a bit like an addiction, and like every real addict, a binge-eater will find a way to be reunited with his substance of abuse; food!!!

Chapter 3

THE ROOT CAUSE OF EMOTIONAL EATING

Yes, we have delved into how people practice emotional eating, but you also need to know why emotional eating becomes an issue in the first place. Now, there is no single cause for binge-eating. Instead, there are a large number of psychological, sociocultural, and biological factors that make it possible and much more likely for you to binge-eat. When these factors first align to make you binge-eat, you may not necessarily even notice that you are bingeing more frequently than usual. It gradually creeps on you until it has eked out a neural path in the brain. Then, it becomes hard to force out.

I have grouped these factors into three; Underlying factors which represent certain dormant risks that can make you predisposed to picking up an eating disorder as BED later in life, risk factors which are current habits that make it likely for you to develop BED and precipitating factors which launch recurrent episodes of binge-eating.

Underlying Factors

These factors are largely beyond your control as they regularly occur at a very young age or due to factors beyond us.

Genetics

Scientific studies have shown that children of parents with BED often develop BED themselves later in life. It is unclear if such children develop BED because they imbibe the habit from observing their parents over time, or if the trait is inherited. This means that parents who binge-eat are likely to raise offspring who will binge-eat as well later in the future.

Societal pressure

Societal norms and values can influence the way we eat. In our world today where the rave is all about "being slim," it is easy to feel a bit of pressure over a "not-so-perfect" figure. These may grow to become the source of a loss of confidence. Disordered anxiety, worry, and depression may then follow to shatter what self-esteem they have left. Such individuals may seek refuge in eating, in a way that is almost similar to the way an alcoholic drowns his grief in the bottles.

Parental impact

Experiences while growing up can firm up the chances of developing an eating disorder. For instance, do you know that entreating a small child to complete his tasks or activities with food can create an emotional dependence on food? Telling a child to get a bar of chocolate as soon as he finishes his homework changes the function of the chocolate. No longer is it just something to be eaten and savored; it becomes a means of exacting happiness for the child. (Again, feeding or encouraging a small child to eat beyond his limits can also make it more probable for him to develop BED when he grows up.)

Growing up in a dysfunctional family

A family may be dysfunctional for a wide range of reasons. It may be so because there is a lack of clear and effective communication between the members of the family. Or it could be because the parents are in constant conflict with each other. Whatever the case, growing up in a dysfunctional family setting can repress a child's ability to express himself/herself. Such a child may turn towards food as a source of refuge.

Childhood bullying

A child that has been subject to bullying may suffer a lot of emotional and mental dysfunction. Such a kid may grow to possess very little-esteem and a lack of self-identity. It is highly likely that such individuals will need external validation to feel good about themselves. In the absence of this external validation, it is not uncommon for them to turn towards bingeing to round the edges of their bruised ego.

Biology

Binge-eating can also occur as a result of a biological quirk in our body. We have talked about the impact of abnormal levels of ghrelin and leptin on the binge cycle. They are not the only two hormones that can twist the normal body reaction to the presence of food. Serotonin and dopamine play a large part too. Abnormally low levels of serotonin, also known as the happiness hormone can cause an individual to take a larger than usual quantity of food before he can feel pleased and satisfied. That means people with this low level of serotonin need to eat more to derive the feelings of satisfaction and fulfillment. That can invariably lay the ground for BED to creep in. Also, dopamine is responsible for the sensation of pleasure that comes with most of our enjoyable habits. It is the hormone of addiction and is responsible for emotional eating. Some people get used to the dopamine rush that accompanies the consumption of food very quickly. For people like that, binge-eating is a classical addiction

Risk Factors for Binge-Eating

In the presence or absence of underlying factors, risk factors broaden the chance an individual has of engaging in binge-eating. Let's look at some of the more common risk factors.

Previous trauma experience

Binge-eating can present as a part of post-traumatic stress disorder. People who have suffered significant traumatic episodes such as the loss of a loved one, sexual abuse or physical violence often develop mental health issues. Binge-eating may develop as a complication of the state of mind they fleet within.

Gender

For reasons unknown, studies have conclusively proven that women binge-eat far more than men. There is a fifty percent greater chance that you are going to binge as a woman than a man. This is yet another risk factor to consider.

Low esteem

By now, it should be reasonably apparent to you that binge-eating seems to have a good lot to do with low self-esteem. Here is the explanation. People with low-esteem think they are not good enough or worthy of their reputation. They continuously cast aspersions on themselves and beat themselves internally over things they couldn't handle. They look up to friends and family members to reassure them and boost their esteem level a bit. Especially when they are already a little bit obese or ashamed of their structure, they may choose to go on a diet simply because they feel compelled to lose weight to fit a particular stereotype. In the long run, because their motivation to lose weight is faulty, they let slip and go on a binge-eating spree. Sure, they feel sorry and unhappy about that later, but low esteem ensures the episodes are going to recur.

Body size

Obese people with their typical larger-than-average body size are more likely to binge than moderately sized people. In the first place, a large percentage of obese people got to that position from overeating. Also, they have a relatively larger food requirement. Now, when you add this to the fact that obese people are usually under some form of societal pressure to lose weight, it is easy to see why they may feel bad about themselves and turn towards overeating for succor.

Inability to express emotions

If you generally have problems expressing your feelings and opinions to other people, including those that are close to you, then you may end up a walking ball of anger and suppressed emotion. For people like that, eating takes their mind off their frustrations. So, they eat whenever they can, and anywhere they can.

Precipitating Factors

Now, we have discussed the first two groups of factors; the last group explains factors that can serve as a form of trigger for you to binge-eat right now.

Pregnancy

Nutritional requirements change during pregnancy, and so does the eating pattern too. For many people, pregnancy comes with a lot of changes in appetite; for a binge-eater, it is the perfect excuse to go an eating spree. The body demands extra food to cater for the unborn child, but this increased appetite can trigger the dormant tendency to binge-eat in a lot of people.

Stress

Stress is perhaps one of the most potent triggers of binge-eating. Naturally, when we are tired, we require rest and sustenance to boost our energy reserves and get the body back to the optimal status. However, beyond even tiredness, emotional and mental stress can also trigger a binge. The first thing a binge-eater turns to when he is stressed out is food. It doesn't matter what the source of stress is. It could be physical fatigue from working all day, the aftermath of a physical confrontation or the manifestation of emotional abuse. Along the same line, codependent individuals are some of the worst binge-eaters around. They turn towards food at each point along the path. Binge-eating brought about by stress is quite thorough, so to speak. It is virtually impossible to stop if you have already made stress a trigger for eating. That is why it is hard for you to stop after the first few bites of that chocolate bar.

Anxiety

Thirty-seven percent of people with an anxiety disorder binge-eat. Anxiety and binge-eating disorder interact in almost the same way as stress interacts with the latter. During anxious or excitable moments, a binge-eater is likely to think of food as a way to stabilize his mental state. This is wrong, of course, as food has nothing to do with emotions. However, anxiety is a good enough excuse for a binge-eater.

Weight-loss programs/dieting

This is the most important factor for binges. No other factor or cause even comes close to it in potency. When you go on a diet or any other weight-loss program, the body is starved of food for some time in the hope of reducing body weight through fasting or cutting down calories. Naturally, this causes the body to crave for food more. The longer and more intensive the fast, the higher the craving for food and the likelier the chance that a binge-eater will break his resolve and binge on everything he can lay his hands upon. For a true binge-eater, starving his body of food for an extended period causes classic withdrawal symptoms such as anxiety, palpitations, a strong urge to eat, and mental stress. No matter how long he may resist the urge to eat, something eventually snaps. He realizes he can eat after all and decides to break his fast or dieting plan. Now, many binge-eaters may even try to convince themselves that they are only going to eat a little and then resume their fast. Alas, that is often a lie. The gates open and they flood their body with excess food until they become physically uncomfortable even.

By way of summary, binge-eating does not have a single cause. Instead, a combination of different factors ranging from childhood habits, genetics, and emotional distress, to dieting can cause the signs of binge-eating to manifest in an individual.

Chapter 4

DO YOU BINGE-EAT?

❋ ❋ ❋ ❋ ❋ ❋ ❋ ❋ ❋ ❋ ❋ ❋ ❋ ❋ ❋ ❋ ❋

When it started over three decades and a half ago, Freda didn't take it too seriously after all she was only just a lanky teenager with too many activities to do, and too little time to spare. All she had to do after a long period of starvation was to curl up on her couch, remote in one hand and feast on anything and everything that came to her imagination. A typical night for her usually begins with a snack and ends with several calories of processed junk going through her mouth, almost notice.

However, just like a drug user gradually descending into a frightening 'low' from an exceeding 'high' state, the guilty feeling that accompanies these moments of excessive eating nauseated her each time. So did the amount of time she wasted each day to sleep off the unnatural feel of fullness. That had been the ritual for close to thirty-five years. From what seemed an innocent, unusual habit, binge-eating had grown to become her secret vice, one that hurt her every day.

Now, she knew the way she ate was not healthy, but it was hard for her to give a name to the pattern because she had no idea anything as binge-eating disorder existed. So many people have faced a similar problem. Because there are no bottles of alcohol or used needles and tourniquets, many do not know if this malaise is an addiction or not. If you are one of those unable to conclude whether they have BED or not, this chapter is for you. The aim is to point out the signs, symptoms, and several other visible but hidden telltale pointers of BED.

Majorly, symptoms of BED can be divided into;

1. **Behavioral** symptoms which include loss of self-control in matters regarding food, eating to stultifying proportions, eating numerous times, during irregular intervals during the day, including but not limited to adopting and quitting different weight loss plans.

2. **Emotional** symptoms which may include shame, unusual stress which can only be relieved by gorging yourself on food and a loss of mindfulness.

We will go through some of the more common signs one after the other.

Behavioral Signs

Loss of control over the amount of food eaten

Loss of control when eating is a feature that is and should be seen only in babies. However, while most babies outgrow that phase of their life, some revisit that mode when they become binge-eaters, later in life. Losing control over the amount and manner in which you eat is one of the most potent and apparent signs of binge eating. It is often a clear sign of BED. A binge-eater may only wish to take a bite or two out of a sandwich, but he finds himself gobbling up the entire sandwich very quickly. This psychological inability to stop eating when you are full is usually a clear sign of BED.

Eating when you are not hungry

When a person is hungry, the ideal thing is for hormones secreted by the body to communicate this uncomfortable sensation to the brain. The brain then makes us aware that we are hungry and in need of sustenance. At this point, we start to seek food to refresh and sustain our body. For a binge-eater, it is ever so slightly different. He gets prompted to eat even when his body does not need refreshment or nourishment at that point. For him, it is a psychological prompt rather than a real biological need to eat.

So, if you consistently find out that you eat even without truly being hungry or you eat even when you are already full, you would do good to consider yourself a prime suspect for BED.

Hiding and stockpiling food for future consumption

As a former binge-eater myself, I know secrecy is a big part of it all. I also planned my binges. At times, I would be at work and start making a list of what to buy on the way home. Naturally, nobody wants to get recognized as being addicted to food, so it became vital for me to add secrecy to my dealings with food. I hoarded snacks, juices and every other junk item you could conceivably find in a store. I stocked my fridge up to ensure I had no excuse to run out of my favorite snacks and drinks. Even after that, though, I still had more hidden away in safe drawers and locations in the pantry. It is that serious an obsession for most binge-eaters too. Secrecy, hoarding, and stockpiling food items out of barely disguised shame is an excellent pointer to the fact that eating has gone beyond a natural process and progressed into an addiction.

Cutting out entire food groups for periods

This is both a sign and a potential cause for binge-eating. Going all out on an anti-carb diet, for instance, is meant to make you lose weight scientifically. However, if you are already addicted to the same carbohydrates you are trying to cut out, there is bound to be a problem. The cravings will rise even more than ever, and psychologically, you may be fighting one war that you are primed to lose. When this cold-turkey approach to quitting a specific class of food snaps, you are bound to feast on the very same thing you have been avoiding more than ever. Sure, the guilt will come later, but if you find yourself consciously or subconsciously cutting out a class of food and deriving severe craving for the same food, it may be a sign that you are an active binge-eater.

Eating numerous times within a day

Many binge-eaters do not need an excuse to cram food down their bellies. A binge-eater eats when he is less busy, busy, stressed, hungry, and when he is happy. In short, eating becomes a one-stop solution to all of his emotional troubles. If you look back at night and realize that you ate more than five, six times a day, then you will agree with me that it seems like you have lost control of your eating pattern.

✱ Adopting and quitting various weight loss plans ✱

How many times have you started a *"magical"* weight loss program only to stop a few weeks later? Not necessarily because you found out, it wasn't working but because you discovered that "Heck, I can't do this no more. Pass me a plate of nachos". Now, binge-eating is not the only reason people quit weight-loss programs, but if you find out that the main reason you are quitting is that your cravings for food seem to outstrip your goals for losing weight, alarm bells should ring.

Some years back, when I was still suffering from BED, I took on the 16/8 intermittent fasting plan that gave me only eight hours to eat in a day. Well, I bore the sixteen hours fast stoically enough for the first few days, but it always seemed to me that I was eating thrice as much in my eight hours window of eating. As each day went past, it became harder and harder not to eat for those sixteen hours. The eight hours seemed to continually remind me of how much eating was pleasurable and gave me a thousand reasons to break the plan. My 16/8 project lasted all of six days before I had a "Heck" moment. After a few weeks, I was ready to go on yet another weight-loss diet. Most binge-eaters face these moments too that ensure that their addiction remains as potent as ever.

Emotional Signs That You Are Binge Eating

There are a wide variety of emotional signs that can mark out a binge-eater as well.

 Unease associated with eating in public

Simply because you might have evolved your unique eating pattern in private, one that involves eating rapidly, you may feel discomfited when you need to eat outside with others. You may not necessarily eat in the same manner in public, but there is bound to be unease stemming from some reserved feeling of shame.

 Stress that is relieved only by eating

What is your first answer when you are stressed? Is it food? What comes to your mind when you are exhausted? Food or rest? If you always choose food as an answer to physical stress, then you are an emotional eater. The key in the last statement is "always," as other people may do the same from time to time. For a binge-eater though, it is food or nothing else.

 Loss of mindfulness while bingeing

Do you sometimes plan your Saturday since Friday night, wake up feeling pumped up, grab a bowl of popcorn, flick on the TV for just a moment, and find yourself still sitting there four hours later? How often does this happen to you? How often do you forget time and your plans while eating? Do you get so carried away that you exist in almost a cocoon surrounded by food? Most binge-eaters experience this loss of mindfulness from time to time.

Feeling extremely body-conscious

Anybody can feel body-conscious for a while, but for a binge-eater, he is painfully aware of how thin or fat he is every minute of the day. He turns his body image into a weapon to batter himself. This consciousness is the product of low-esteem as we discuss further in chapter five. Binge-eating enforces a negative self-image upon you and makes you body-conscious in a very negative way. It is one of its most critical signs.

A lack of satiety

During binges, you will never feel full if you are a binge eater. Or perhaps more accurately, you will not notice the feeling. A binge-eater may find it hard to stop eating even when he is full. The problem arises from the fact that he isn't eating to satisfy hunger. So, when his body tells him he is no longer hungry, he disregards the knowledge and keeps eating. An average individual can tell when he is full and can cease to eat; it is almost an impossible task for a binge-eater to do the same. So, if you find it hard to tell the right time to leave the table, you should watch out for more signs of binge-eating disorder.

Guilt and depression after eating

Nobody should have to feel guilty or depressed after eating, but binge-eaters do. This feeling is perhaps the most distinguishing feature of binge-eating from other eating disorders. If you eat so much that you get disgusted or unhappy with the fact, the chances are indeed sky-high that you are a binge-eater.

These are the significant signs that can point out a binge-eating problem when they appear together. Let us go one step further though and examine a more structured diagnosis model for BED.

Diagnosis of BED

Binge Eating Disorder is not just some fancy English word for overeating. Instead, it is an actual mental disorder as evidenced by its eventual appearance in the DSM V in 2013. The DSM is the world's accepted manual for psychiatric disorders. Before it was finally listed, BED was under EDNOS (Eating Disorder Not Otherwise Specified), a category of eating disorders that are not entirely understood. However, with its placement in DSM V, BED has attained more consciousness and attention in the psychiatry and self-care fields. More importantly, the DSM has set aside criteria for determining if you have a binge-eating disorder or not.

The DSM criteria state that for BED to be confirmed, overeating should occur in association with,

- -A Loss of control,

- -Emotional imbalance after binges and

- -Physical distress after eating, for three months (at least once a week).

Each of these criteria must be present before a diagnosis of overeating can be correct. Just as important, the DSM also states that at least three of the following must be present at the same time as the criteria above.

- Eating more frequently and rapidly

- Eating till discomfort sets in

- Guilt, and depression over bingeing episodes

- Eating while not hungry

- Regularly eating alone

It is also essential to ensure that there is a lack of compensatory measures such as purging and induced vomiting. If these are present, then the diagnosis tends towards Bulimia Nervosa rather than BED. It is vital to note this difference.

Luckily, binge-eating may start innocuously before creeping up to become a major bad habit, but at least, its diagnosis is quite straightforward. Even before you get to know of the DSM criteria shortly, as a binge-eater, I expect you would understand and acknowledge the fact that you have an eating problem.

Chapter 5

WHY YOU SHOULD NOT BINGE-EAT

If you are a binge-eater, then you acknowledge that you must have known that there was a need for you to stop the habit before picking up this book. At the very least, you have shown understanding that you realize that your binge episodes need to stop. Getting rid of binge-eating is not that straightforward, though. As a real psychological disorder, it goes beyond just the realms of nutrition, deficiencies, and physical discomfort. It also brings attendant social problems, health problem, and possibly personality disorders.

This chapter aims to give you further reasons and motivation to get rid of binge-eating now. Let us take a look at some of the ill-effects of binge-eating.

Weight gain

This is perhaps the main reason why most people with BED seek to get rid of it. Binge-eating confers on you a first-class ticket to excessive weight gain in very short order. It is an express route to pile on extra pounds of flesh that you would be better off not gaining. How binge-eating leads to weight gain is an entire chapter on its own, but for now, let me show you the statistics that say you are likely to gain weight if you are binge-eating.

A conservative estimate puts the figure of people that are on weight loss programs due to BED at forty percent. That means for every ten individual that starts a weight loss program; four could have stopped themselves the stress by discarding binge-eating a long time ago. Even more incriminatingly, as high as twenty percent of all obese people can trace their weight problems to bingeing.

A study by Walden Behavioral Care Center theorizes that the average amount of calories consumed by binge-eaters per episode is 3,415. In addition, twenty percent of people with BED will consume 5,000 calories in a typical episode. Ten percent will consume approximately 6,000 calories in a single episode. These figures serve to illustrate just how badly binge-eating skews the amount of food (in calories) that you may consume in a day. Of course, the excess food will do only one thing; blow your weight out of proportion.

With the excessive increase in weight comes a whole list of weight issues. If for any reason, excessive weight gain is a primary candidate for why you should not make binge-eating a recurrent habit for you.

Even with people who do not gain weight despite binge-eating, there is a danger. It is typical for such people to believe that since they are not overweight, there is no need to seek treatment. This leaves the disorder to exacerbate. Therefore, regardless of your weight range, BED still poses a danger to your general wellbeing.

Loss of self-esteem

As with many of its effects and causes, it is hard to appropriately determine if it is low self-esteem that causes binge eating, or a loss of esteem is only a symptom of binge-eating. However, what is very sure is that binge-eating and a loss of self-respect always walk together hand-in-hand. As I mentioned in chapter three, BED goes beyond just the nutritional problems it causes; it also brings real personality problems. In a perpetual vicious cycle, a binge-eater is likely to feel angry and stupid for overeating. These negative emotions give rise to a usually vitriolic self-tirade that does nothing to improve self-worth. Bingeing leaves you feeling helpless and unworthy of a healthy lifestyle. It leaves you feeling inferior for not being able to exert any control over what you put in your mind. Especially when the ill effects such as weight gain and health problems start to arise, you are almost unable to forgive yourself. Sadly, not even the reduced esteem can force one off the wagon. In most cases, it deepens it.

Eat, feel disgusted with yourself, promise to change, eat in excess again, feel even more troubled, and then turn to food to feel better. It continues like that with each episode further shaving off some of the self-esteem you should be enjoying. The only way to end the disgust, and destroy the inferiority complex is to get rid of binge-eating.

Social awkwardness

This is a by-product of low self-esteem brought about by overeating. Having a negative image of yourself often spills over to the way you handle yourself in public and social encounters. Our external body language is built to mirror the internal feelings we have. Therefore, if binge-eating is taking a hammer to your mental health and confidence, it is bound to show up negatively in the way you interact with others. This exacerbates further when such encounters occur around the time you just binged. Bingeing often happens under an air of secrecy too, and the levels of uneasiness from your eating sessions can spill over to the first few social encounters you get after it.

Lower levels of productivity

An imbalanced mental state automatically translates to lower levels of productivity at work. Add to that the fact that physical discomfort that follows binges can render you unfit for work for some time and BED provides economic impact too. The *Health Economics* undertook a research to compare productivity levels in obese people and individuals that fall within a normal weight range. The results were instructing. The income of obese people was down 2.5% when compared to people with normal body weight. In any case, keeping up binge-eating is surely going to rack up some extra bills on food and consumables with time.

Digestion problems

Our body is built to specification. It has limits to what it can take and process at once. Food undergoes a sophisticated process that leads to its digestion and eventual absorption for use. However, BED disturbs this system. By eating so much food within a short period of time, you get to overwhelm this system and cause it to function at less than optimal conditions. Acid reflux, for instance, is more common with binge-eaters. The excess food too can rob you of efficient digestion and cause constipation. At the same time, rapid gastric emptying where the body gets rid of most of the food you have consumed without processing it for nutrients is likelier with binge-eating. I am trying to tell you that binge-eating does your digestion process no favors.

Physical discomfort

There is no point over-flogging this issue. We all know just how comfortable our stomachs can feel when we overeat. Pain, rumbling, and distension of the abdomen are not the most favorable outcomes that should accompany eating, but excessive food comes with that.

Health issues

If you are not trying to stop binge-eating because of weight, then the chances are high that you are trying to stop BED because of the inherent health risks it comes along with. Think obesity and the health complications it comes with, then give same to binge-eating disorder. Consider low self-esteem and the wrong health-affecting lifestyle choices it can provide and ascribe the same to binge eating. Binge eating affects your health in some of the ways below;

-Cardiovascular problems

Think the heart and the cardiovascular system. Then, think excessive damage to them if you keep up binge-eating. Cardiovascular diseases and conditions such as heart attacks, hypertension, and stroke are the leading causes of death worldwide, and diet contributes a lot to their development. Binge-eating causes an overall increase in the level of triglycerides, cholesterol, and total body fat content, all indices that raise the chance of developing a sudden heart attack. Forget the technical language; all I am saying is the more you binge-eat, the higher your chances of having cardiovascular challenges.

-Diabetes mellitus

Diabetes mellitus, the most common biochemical disease on the planet today, especially type 2 diabetes, is closely allied to obesity. Binge-eating being one of the primary drivers of obesity, therefore, occupies a special place in the list of risk factors for developing Non-insulin dependent Diabetes Mellitus (NIDDM). Things are made worse by the fact that a large part of what you may be eating is going to be sugary. That only throws up a whole vista of other problems.

-Sleep disorders

Binge-eating can lead you towards the development of sleep disorders. First up is sleep apnea. The bigger you get due to BED, the harder it is going to be to keep your throat free while you sleep. Obese binge-eaters often have problems keeping their airways unblocked while they sleep, causing them to snore while they sleep and frequent breaks in sleep. On a psychological level, when you binge at night, it is quite possible for you to find it harder than usual to fall asleep no thanks to physical discomfort and the itch to consume more.

-*Irritable Bowel Syndrome*

IBS and other absorption disorders, such as ulcerative colitis, are more common in people with BED. Explanations have been inconclusive about why this is so, but what is sure is that as a binge-eater, you are more likely to have absorption disorders than the average individual out there.

-*Substance abuse*

One might ask how substance abuse can be a side effect of binge-eating, but it is. Depression and low-esteem that follows BED around ensure that sufferers are never too far away from destructive implosions such as picking up substance abuse. The lure of substance and alcohol abuse to shore up the failing levels of esteem often trap many a binge-eater. Combined with excessive overeating, substance abuse further potentiates the self-destructive tendencies within binge-eaters.

Binge-eating, in its own right, serves as a genuine purveyor of various health, social and mental problems or people addicted to food. When it is closely allied to obesity, depression, and their attendant complications, the list of issues it brings triples and becomes almost endless.

Chapter 6

HOW BINGE-EATING LEADS TO WEIGHT GAIN

Let me start this chapter with some stat facts that bring home the danger that obesity is. From the 1970s till now, the prevalence of obesity has quadrupled many times over. In 2008, for instance, approximately two hundred million men and three hundred million women, over twenty years were estimated to be grossly obese. A decade after, the numbers were three hundred million males and four hundred and fifty females.

The numbers associated with being overweight are even crazier. In the US, not less than thirty percent of adults above twenty years are above the recommended weight limit for their age and height. These numbers have delineated how obesity moved from the fringes of social consciousness to become a frontline topic in the fitness and health industries. Go back three centuries ago, and you will find out that obesity and being fat occupied a different place in society.

Three hundred years ago, most societies considered obesity a mark of affluence, a rich man's problem along with other conditions such as gouty arthritis. The progress of science and researches have shown obesity for what it truly is, a marker of poor health and nutrition. Unfortunately, despite increased awareness, obesity and weight-gain remain murky issues for most to overcome. This is showcased in the ever-increasing number of people battling weight issues. In the previous chapters, we have established that binge-eating makes it more likely that you are going to gain weight, but how does that happen exactly?

To understand this, let us take a bird's eye-view of weight gain. At birth, we are all smaller, miniature versions of the adults we eventually grow into. From the moment we are born though, our body is in energy overdrive, trying to increase our body mass from the food and nutritional supplements we consume. As toddlers, the body's metabolic process is primarily focused on physical and mental development. So, barring any disease, we continue to increase in overall body size and weight exponentially. Growth and development in these early stages are rapid and very noticeable. Our physical development hits a lag phase however, once we clock the first few years of adulthood.

At this moment, the body is no longer on a space-filling mission. Growth under normal circumstances is less rapid and controlled, and you can maintain the same weight range for a longer period, lasting years sometimes. The body has hit a stable equilibrium, and from then on, your lifestyle choices are going to determine your weight majorly. Your body no longer goes on a body-building mission automatically. It doesn't take every morsel of food and try to turn it into a building block for your physical uplift.

Yet, it is at this precise stage that a lot of people make the mistakes that push them onto obesity. It is possible even as a toddler or teenager, to be obese, but it is really in the early stages of adulthood that our choices begin to count toward weight gain or loss. For one, it is then that most people assume responsibility for their life choices. By the end of teenage-hood, the only way you are going to either enjoy marked increase or decrease is in your choice of nutrition and the amount of physical activity you get. From birth to early adulthood, the way we develop can be likened to laying a foundation. The body develops a base framework for us to build upon. After that, you can then choose to go the way you want with your choice of nutrition and physical activity key factors.

Most people do not pay attention to what they are eating. So, it is easy to balloon out of shape, especially in the presence of genetic tendencies to do so. Still, some will continue to eat without adding any extra weight? How does this happen? We will need to do a bit of mathematics to get to the root of that.

What determines if you are going to add or lose weight is the calorie balance. I will explain it. When we consume food, the food gets digested starting from the mouth. It undergoes further digestive processes in the stomach before being absorbed into our bloodstream where it functions to generate energy. Now, the energy generated per weight of a particular food substance is measured in calories. To carry out any process at all, our body needs some energy which it burns off. This energy is also measured in calories. Therefore, the food we take in represents the channel by which we get calories of energy for use. The work we do and physical activity represents an avenue for burning off those calories. At all times, there is going to be a net balance of calories between input and output.

If the balance is in favor of calorie input, i.e., if you are consuming more calories than you burn, your body is going to convert the extra source of calories into fat for future use. That is going to cause a slight increase in the tendency to add weight. If you keep up that balance in favor of calorie input, then there is a real chance that you get to add weight.

If the balance, however, is on the output side, then you require even more energy. Your body is more likely to burn stored food to generate more energy — this burning of stored food and fat results in a loss in wet weight. With constant repetition, it translates to weight loss.

To simplify,

Weight gain is going to occur when energy expenditure (output) is lower than calorie intake

Weight loss occurs when energy expenditure is (output) is greater than the input.

The two statements are the laws guarding weight gain under normal circumstances. What are the normal circumstances?

Have you ever heard of Basal Metabolic Rate, BMR? Well, the BMR is the least amount of energy that your body requires to function at rest. Assume that you are resting or at sleep. Your body continues to burn energy in these relaxed states to keep vital functions and organs such as the heart and brain functioning. So, at all points, you must have enough energy to cover your BMR and any extra work you may need to do. Now, our bodies are never equal by demands. BMR values differ from individual to individual. It even has nothing to do with body mass. Apparently, people with low BMR have lower energy requirements. They are therefore more likely to pile on the pounds if they eat excessively. A person with high BMR has higher demands for energy. Even when they eat a comparatively large meal, their body taps most of the calories in the food and consume it to keep the BMR steady. The remaining calories are consumed by other bodily activities. Therefore, they do not have excess calories to store as fat.

How does BMR relate to weight gain and loss? The explanation simply means that people with high BMR values burn more energy and are less likely to gain weight compared to those with low BMRs. That is why your friend seems always to polish off mountains of food but remains as lean as he wants to. You, on the other hand, may feel like every single thing you eat goes directly to hang from your abdomen as belly fat. The difference in BMR is the reason why some people gain weight easily while others do not.

Now, how may binge-eating interplay with all these variables to mark you out as a prime candidate for excessive weight-gain? The primary problem, as you may have inferred, is with the number of calories you get to consume as a binge-eater. As I mentioned in chapter five, for instance, a typical binge-eater consumes about three to four thousand calories per meal. What does the body do with this sudden influx of food that it does not necessarily need? Of course, there is only much the body can get rid of as waste products. Instead, most of the extra calories go into the body as stored fats, which is a basis for massive weight gain.

Therefore, binge-eating is a potent tool for weight gain, especially when it is allied with a lack of physical activity. That is why binge-eaters are more likely to gain weight. It accounts for the important role that binge-eating plays in obesity demographics. It distorts the calories balance equation in favor of the intake. That leaves the body with far more energy and food than it needs. There is only one scenario in that case.

Besides its disturbance of the calorie balance equation, how else may binge-eating affect weight gain?

Spike and dump syndrome
Binge-eaters are not the smartest or most conscionable eaters. They often crave for a certain class of food and go straight to consume it in large, rapid quantities. Carbohydrates (sugar) occupy a special place of honor in the list of most common foods that binge-eaters abuse their bodies with. Unfortunately, for all the good it does our body, eating carbohydrates, especially in excess or rapidly, changes the metabolism of the body.

Carbohydrate's digestion starts from the mouth via saliva. In the stomach, concentrated acid works on the partially digested food. After digestion, carbohydrate now converted into glucose is taken into the bloodstream as a source of energy. There, the movement of glucose into the cells for uptake is regulated by a hormone, insulin. Usually, the uptake of glucose by the cells is gradual and unhurried. When binge-eating forces you to consume a large number of carbs though, that's an entirely different issue. It causes what is known as the Spike-and-dump syndrome.

In this situation, instead of the new glucose in your bloodstream getting introduced gradually, there is a gigantic spike in blood glucose levels due to the large quantity of food you ate. This glucose jump does not last for long, though. Sensitized by the spike, the body produces a large amount of insulin to counter the glucose. This enhanced production soon comes to haunt you, though. The excess insulin causes the blood glucose level to fall below normal. In its bid to bring down the soaring values, insulin overworks and leads to a general crash in glucose levels. This means that when you eat carbohydrates in large quantities, you get an artificial increase in glucose known as a spike. This spike tells the body to produce more insulin. During this period, you may experience a false sugar high and observe that you are slightly overactive and energetic. The feeling doesn't last though before the glucose crash sends you into a less excited, irritable state. This can easily turn into a vicious cycle that increases your tendency to binge-eat.

You may either get addicted to the initial sugar high that you get and that increases your cravings for more food. Or the crash gets you feeling lousy and in need of a mood enhancer. A true binge-eater will turn to food again. Therefore, through its promotion of the spike and crash syndrome, binge-eating makes it likely that you are going to eat more than is necessary.

Rapid Gastric emptying

Binge-eating also causes rapid gastric emptying. Food that is eaten remains within the stomach for some hours before it is moved into the intestine to be absorbed. Binge-eating disorganizes this by causing the stomach to empty its bowels too early and rapidly ahead of schedule.

Let me explain it this way. Your kitchen sink has a drain that allows small food particles like grains to pass through it even though they are not meant to be poured there in the first place. These little particles continue to go through the drain as long as they remain in small quantities. Force a large amount of these particles down the drain, and there will be a temporary blockage of passage. Even water may not be able to flow past that until you clear the mess. Our gastrointestinal tract acts in almost the same way.

When we overeat, instead of forcing itself to process the food, the digestive system sometimes takes the easy way out by dumping the whole meal and marking it for evacuation and disposal. Have you noticed that when you eat beyond your limits, you only feel full for about two to three hours maximum before hunger sets in again? Well, that is because your stomach has rapidly emptied its contents. With binge-eating, a lot of what you eat is going to pass through your bowels undigested. That means you will not be able to take full nutrients from what you eat. You will also get hungry quite quickly and need a helping or supporting dose of food for each unannounced binge.

Why you should be wary of gaining excess weight

I have explained the concept of BMI, calorie balance, rapid gastric emptying, and the spike-and-crash syndrome as examples of how binge-eating can make you gain unneeded weight. Now, why shouldn't you gain excess fat? I have mentioned some cardinal points why a large weight gain is detrimental to your health and overall well-being; I'll add more in this chapter.

Before we go further, though, I should stress that not all weight gain is bad. It all depends on your current weight with respect to your age and height. It is a commonplace for people to abhor weight gain and seek to starve themselves into weight reduction. However, there is such a thing as being dangerously underweight too. Having a lower than normal weight could also signal deeper issues and needs rectification as well.

Calculating BMI

To help you answer the question of whether you need to lose weight or not, the Body Mass Index, BMI is key. It is a mathematical formula that takes into account your height to check if your body weight falls within a healthy range for your height.

To calculate your own BMI, you need to divide your weight in kilogram by the square of your height in meters. The unit is Kg/m^2.

Let us take a brief example;

If your weight is 80 kilograms and your height is 1.74 meters, then your BMI is 80kg divided by the square of 1.74meters. The BMI will be equal to 26.0 Kg/m^2.

Let us see how to interpret BMI results.

- A BMI value of less than 18 is considered low and suggestive that the individual is underweight. The lower the BMI, the more essential it is to put on more weight. Most people with anorexia are found with less than 18 in BMI values.

- A healthy BMI result should fall within 18.5 and 24.9. A BMI within this range says your weight is okay.

- BMI values within 25.0 and 29.9 suggest that the individual in question is overweight already and should be looking to lose weight.

- A value above 30 represents full-blown obesity. At this range, it is important that medication, exercise, and a customized diet be applied to cause an immediate reduction in weight.

Limitations of BMI

BMI is the most reliable indicator to assess body weight range, but it does have some drawbacks too.

BMI monitors weight and not fat. That means it cannot differentiate what percentage of your total weight is fat that you need to be rid of, and which part is pure muscle. For well-built, muscled people, the BMI can flag a false-positive for weight loss. For instance, a bodybuilder with significant muscle mass may have the same BMI as an average individual of the same weight and height. Of course, the bodybuilder may have more muscle than fat and does not need any weight loss. At the same time, the average individual may have a lot of fat and need weight loss. However, BMI values may suggest that the bodybuilder needs to lose some weight or vice versa.

By the same logic, BMI does not consider pregnancy. Normally, during pregnancy, women gain weight. If the BMI is taken, the values will be skewed due to this increase in weight. Therefore, a pregnant woman may be flagged in error as needing to lose weight.

This is the major limitation of BMI, but still, it remains a reliable check of weight suitability.

Now, let us look at more reasons why you should not gain weight, especially if you do not need to adjust yet.

Poor health

I have already listed some health complications that can arise from obesity, but it is pertinent that I still hammer upon this point.

Increased risks of cancers.

Gaining extra weight above a certain range can leave you open to a higher risk of colon, breast, and prostate cancers. Studies have shown that obese people are more likely to come down with these particular cancers compared to people with moderate weight.

Fatty liver syndrome

This is one syndrome that is not fully understood in the medical world just yet. The livers of sufferers get inflamed, swollen, and take on a fatty look. This makes it function at a less-than-optimal state and may eventually lead to cirrhosis. It is similar to alcoholic liver disease, but its causes are unknown. What has been proven though is that obese and overweight people with excessive belly fat are more prone to come down with the syndrome?

Pregnancy complications

Pregnancy is usually associated with weight gain logically as you have a fetus growing in within you. There are also a lot of bodily changes going on that could lead to what should be a transient gain in weight. Nevertheless, pregnancy and rapid weight gain do not go along smoothly. In the first instance, overweight and obese people are more likely to develop gestational diabetes. This is a form of diabetes that occurs during pregnancy. By the same logic, an overweight pregnant woman has higher odds of experiencing high blood pressure, which manifests as preeclampsia. These do not bode well for the health of both the growing fetus and the mother.

Acute weight gain during pregnancy can also increase the chances of giving birth to pre-term babies. These are babies who get delivered prematurely before the usual thirty-six weeks of pregnancy is complete. Babies of overweight mothers have also been demonstrated to have a higher chance of being obese in the future as well. Further research has also shown that the incidence of stillbirths is more common among the obese. As if that is not enough, overeating during pregnancy till you gain too much weight is unlikely to help you return to shape after you have given birth. The effects of a weight gain are keenly felt postpartum. Therefore, during pregnancy, adequate care should be paid to weight gain to ensure it is kept within limits.

Osteoarthritis and other joint problems

With age, the integrity of our joint declines due to frequent wear and tear caused by constant movement. Osteoarthritis typifies these joint problems, but majorly, most joint problems develop with advancing age or physical trauma. Obesity changes the entire landscape, though. Acute weight gain places further burden and stress on joints, especially the hip, waist, and elbow joints. This can cause the joints to wear off faster than usual and lead to osteoarthritis quicker. Especially when you have a slender frame before, weight gain can have a marked effect on joint integrity. This is because the joints have already developed to bear a certain range of weight. Then, suddenly, your new weight asks them to take on even more load than they are built for.

Rapid weight gain causes you to gain more fat than muscle

Healthy weight-gain is a paced, slow process that ensures that you are packing on actual muscle rather than fat. Rapid weight-gain as caused by binge-eating, on the other hand, adds on mostly unhealthy fat. A healthy weight gain shouldn't exceed 0.5-0.8 pounds per week. Anything above that and you risk piling on the fats rather than the muscles you ideally want. The general consensus is that body fat percentage should not exceed 25% in men and 35% in women.

Physical fitness

There is a reason athletes are probably the fittest group of people in the world; they remain as lean as possible with next to no excess fat. This allows them to maximize their full physical potentials. By remaining at an optimal weight, you are going to find it easier to perform physical activities without getting fatigued easily. Inordinate weight gain robs you of your fitness.

Depletion of Self-confidence

It is a shame and highly pathetic, but there is no denying that body-shaming has come to stay in our society today. Via the Web and mass media, every single person on this planet is connected to every other person on the planet. Every day, we get bombarded by other people's opinion, thoughts, and ideas. Unfortunately, when it comes to weight loss and gain, the society is screaming that obesity is to be avoided at all cost. Public perception says that being fat is very wrong. There are crude, insensitive remarks and jokes everywhere about fat people. This stereotype has therefore reinforced a lack of self-confidence onto the minds of most overweight people.

As an obese individual, you may begin to feel inadequate and insecure with your body. You are extra sensitive to negative remarks, and often, any comment about obesity seems directed at you. And there are plenty of those every day. Shows, beauty pageants, and talk-shows are produced each day to reinforce the belief that a perfect individual is a slim, lean individual.

With time, all these inputs grow to devastate the self-esteem of overweight people. If binge-eating gets you fat, then you can expect that it is going to feed fat on your self-esteem and confidence. You are already familiar with the relationship between depression and binge-eating. All these coalesce to ensure that you begin to feel less-worthy of respect from others.

To end this chapter, it is evident by now that binge-eating has a lot to do with weight gain. It provides the surplus substrate from which the body may explode into obesity. To combat the ill-effects of obesity and rapid weight gain, it is essential to deal with binge-eating as soon as possible.

PART TWO

DEFEATING BINGE EATING

Here in part three, the focus is on overcoming binge-eating. There are major approaches to treating an individual with binge-eating disorder, but the most effective are weight-loss therapy and cognitive behavioral therapy. Chapter seven deals with weight loss therapy via nutrition. The idea is to give you a clear idea of what you should be eating as a binge-eater to reduce your chances of suffering a binge episode.

Chapter eight and nine deal with the twin dangers of sugar and processed foods. These are two classes of food that may promote binge-eating, especially when they are consumed in excess. Chapter ten discusses cognitive behavioral therapy, another very effective approach to getting rid of binge-eating.

Chapter Eleven focuses on other treatment approaches to include Family-Based Therapy, Motivation to Change Therapy, and Dialectical Behavioral Therapy. The last chapter contains essential tips that cover exercise, meditation, confidence, and eating tips to round up the whole book and tie all loose ends.

Chapter 7

WEIGHT LOSS THERAPY

What To Eat

There is no denying the fact that a lot of binge-eaters are fixated on losing weight. This is so since the greater proportion of obese people belong to the BED group than any other group. In what appears to be quite a conundrum, the foremost weapon of choice against excess weight gain today seems to be dieting. That throws a cat among the pigeons when you consider the fact that the number one cause/trigger of binge-eating is going on a diet or starving yourself.

The first rule to throw to a binge-eater is, "Do not starve, go on a prolonged fast or adopt a stringent diet." This is because the longer you starve yourself, the stronger your cravings to eat finally. It is like damming a full river back. Eventually, when the gates are released, you are likely to flood your system with too much food. So, there, we have already established that starving or dieting can be a bad thing for you if you are a binge-eater.

Now, we need to answer the question, "how do I lose weight as a binge-eater." Let me be frank and honest here. Going on and adhering to a weight-loss diet is a very effective means of losing weight. Unfortunately, it is not the path you want to go down as a binge-eater because it will backfire and come to register as a medium for gaining unneeded, excess weight. So, what is the way forward? How can you keep your weight in check as a binge-eater?

The only sure way is to change your nutrition and the way you eat. You need new eating habits and ideas that can ensure that you do not pile on extra weight. You need to inculcate new dietary choices that make it more likely that you are going to shed off some existing weight with the right kind of exercise. For you, as a binge-eater, it is not about how many times you eat. It is about what you are eating. It is not about how well you can starve yourself. It has to be about how nourished you are. Don't have to starve self

With that in mind, weight loss therapy for a binge-eater focuses on eating the right classes of food that ensure you are less likely to go on a binge, and how to eat them. That will be our focus in this chapter. Let us start with the individual classes of food, and see what you should and should not eat.

Carbohydrates

Carbohydrates are at once the most common food item and potentially the most dangerous class of food that can feature heavily in a binge-eaters diet. Carbohydrates provide us with the glucose we need for our daily activities. They are the primary source of energy for bodily functions. However, carbohydrates need to be eaten with care if they are not to cause havoc to you.

How can you eat carbohydrate correctly? Carbohydrates can be grouped into two depending on their glycemic index. The glycemic index is an indicator of how much glucose a food substance holds and how fast it releases it into the bloodstream. Starchy carbohydrate such as rice, pasta, and white bread have a high glycemic index should be avoided. These carbs are digested to release inordinately large amounts of glucose. Remember the spike-and-dump syndrome? Starchy carbohydrates are the most potent activators of the syndrome. Instead, your goal should be carbohydrates of the other group, with a low glycemic index. You do not need to cut out starchy carbohydrates totally, but you must keep them in moderation. In small amounts, starchy carbohydrates are best consumed early in the morning to provide the body's requirement for energy early in the day. On the same level, fibrous foods like fruits contain some glucose too and are generally better sources of carbohydrates than starchy foods.

Mostly, grains are the best bet among carbohydrates. Grains, such as barley, oats, and rye are digested to release glucose at a much steadier, slower rate that meets the body's requirement for energy without causing severe changes in sugar level. However, there is a catch to eating whole grains too. Typically, a grain consists of three layers; the germ layer (that contains fats, carbs, proteins, vitamins, and antioxidants), endosperm (that contains carbohydrate and proteins) and bran (fibers, antioxidants, and minerals). However, processing procedures such as threshing and milling can lead to a loss of the bran. This greatly reduces the number of nutrients available per gram.

Therefore, unprocessed, whole grains are the best form of carbohydrates to consume. However, refined grains constitute the bulk of the carbohydrate options available today. White flour and pastries, for instance, are derivatives gotten from processed grains. Unprocessed grains, on the other hand, retain all three of their layers and are able to offer up more vitamins and minerals when compared against processed grains.

Fiber from fruits and vegetables.

Fibers are a class of food that is often criminally underrated in nutritional therapy. Fiber, usually gotten from fruits and vegetables, primarily ease bowel movement. Beyond that though, they have a purely mechanical role in the eradication of binge-eating disorder. Fibrous foods are generally filling, and just a little quantity of them is required to fill up your stomach. What that means is that you get to eat less when you eat fibrous foods. They also contain little calories, and the sugar within them is of the low glycemic index type. So, by adding one or two oranges and a slice of pineapple, you can fill up your stomach quickly and reduce the amount of food you are consuming.

Besides, fruits and vegetables offer you a very large variety of choices. You can choose from citrus, berries, melons, or any other group of fruits. With different flavors and taste options, you can hardly go wrong with a selection of fruit. Vegetables also come in different types such as roots and leafy vegetables.

Aside from the fiber, fruits and vegetables are high in vitamin content than most other food substances. Vitamins C, E, and micronutrients such as magnesium and folic acid can be easily gotten from consuming fruits and vegetables. Fruits also contain phytochemicals which boost metabolism within the body and reduce the risk of diseases such as persistent hypertension. Most importantly, for a binge-eater, fruits and vegetables contain very low calories.

Therefore, if you must binge on something, they offer you a safer alternative than the sugar-laden options you may already be used to.

Fat

Carbohydrates may be the most vilified food class in the market today, but fats and oils occupy a close second. It is understandable that since fats and oils generally function primarily in bulking up the body, they will be fingered as major culprits in weight gain. However, this is both true and untrue at the same time.

Fats and oils are the most complex class of food, and their roles are often misunderstood. On the one hand, they are the primary components of cell membranes, offer insulation against rapid changes in the external temperature and also act as cofactors in the absorption of some vitamins, such as Vitamin D for instance. Besides that, few people know that fats contribute a lot to energy production in the body. In fact, they generate more energy per weight than carbohydrates. However, because the brain prefers glucose as its source of energy, fats are usually just stored to perform other physiological functions.

On the other hand, too many fats, especially unhealthy fats, can lead to adverse effects in the body. Excess fats consumption can result in an increase in HDL cholesterol, which is the primary risk factor for some cardiovascular diseases such as atherosclerosis and even heart attacks. Therefore, for a binge-eater, it is important to consume fats in moderate amounts. But even more importantly, only the right kinds of fats and oils must be consumed. Let me clarify better.

As a rule, foods high in fats represent some of the most attractive options on most tables. Think grilled meat, pastries, and fries. Other foods high in fat content include milk, cheese, animal products in general, macrons, margarine, popcorn, and fishes with high-fat content such as salmon and trout. All forms of oil present in our diets also belong to this food class. Palm oil, vegetable oil, olive oil, and safflower oil are only some of them. Now, from this teeming variety of fats, which fats should you consume more.

Generally, there are three main types of fats; monounsaturated, polyunsaturated, and saturated fats. Monounsaturated fats represent the healthiest choice of fats for a binge-eaters diet. Examples of food that contain monounsaturated fats are nuts, fishes, and vegetable oils. Unfortunately, most people consume more fats from other classes of fats. This poses significant health risks and increases the occurrence of binge episodes.

The saturated fats are especially risky for your health. Examples include palm oil, butter, whole milk, and cream. Polyunsaturated fats are mostly found in pastries and microwave-processed foods in general. For a binge-eater, the focus should be on reducing fats and oils to a bare minimum in the diet. If you must take fats, then make sure you are going for the healthiest option. For instance, skimmed milk, a monounsaturated fat, can adequately replace whole milk, a polyunsaturated fat, in your diet.

What Should Drink

What you drink as a recovering binge-eater is just as important as the things you eat and consume daily. It is almost impossible to go through a binge without accompanying excessive consumption of fluids. Unfortunately, most of the fluids people end up drinking on a binge do more harm than good. So, what should you drink and what should you limit?

Water

Water is the most abundant material substance on the planet and in our bodies. It performs so many functions that it is literally impossible to function well when there is some issue with adequate water consumption. It is essentially the major component needed for nutrient transportation in the form of blood. For you as a binge-eater, it is doubly important to consume as much water as possible because of water,

-Brings faster satiety; a glass of water can fill your belly quicker than most other food items. It will keep you from overeating beyond a certain level at the very least. Each time you get a binge trigger, drinking enough water can suppress your desire to eat appreciably. Even if it doesn't succeed, at the very least, it will reduce the quantity of food you can eat.

-*Decreases cravings;* it has been proven that cravings for sugary and fizzy drinks increase significantly when the body is dehydrated. This means that if you do not drink enough water, you are more likely to resort to carbonated drinks or other unhealthy options to fulfill your thirst. Therefore, drink enough water to prevent thirst-fueled binges on soft drinks and alcohol.

-*Flushes the system*; Excess water is filtered out at the kidneys when needed. You can engage this mechanism to get rid of potentially toxic and harmful substances you may have ingested. By drinking water in excess, your body system gets flushed and eliminates toxin faster. Consider it as a form of a hard reset for your body system.

-*Keeps you hydrated;* Hydration is a key component of binge avoidance. A dehydrated individual is more likely to get fatigued easily, frustrated, and in search of a quick energy boost. All these combine to put you at a greater risk of bingeing. You can eliminate the risk by drinking water insufficiently adequate quantities.

At the very least, it is recommended that everybody drink four to five liters of water every day. Allow the upper limit to be your own starting point as a binge-eater. Drink a minimum of five liters of water every day to reduce the chances of you engaging in a binge episode and keep your body prim and hydrated.

Alcohol

Findings state that about 185 billion dollars are lost to alcoholism yearly. An approximate 12% of Americans are also reported to be struggling with an alcohol issue. How does alcoholism affect binge-eating?

To start with, alcoholism itself is a form of binge-eating. Let us look at its features. Not everyone that drinks alcohol is an alcoholic, of course. However, alcoholism is typified by being irrevocably attracted to intoxicating drinks by way of coping with an emotional situation or as a habit. Whereas the general definition describes of BED as a phenomenon characterized by a loss of control over food and emotional eating, alcoholism can be substituted for food in every definition of BED that I know.

An alcoholic often has an issue he should face and resolve. Instead, he hides behind the bottles and drowns his fears and emotions in alcohol. Episodes are then often followed by a deep sense of shame and guilt. That does not stop him from getting flat-out drunk the very next day.

You will agree with me that it is hard not to tar alcoholism with the same brush as binge-eating. In both cases, food and alcohol are certainly not problems. Instead, a loss of control over the quantity to be consumed and when to consume them is the issue. Besides that, excess alcohol potentiates weight gain and binge-eating quite effectively. It is no surprise to see expressions such as a "drinker's belly" commonly used in relation with alcoholics. How can laying off the bottle help you as a form of weight therapy, especially when you are addicted to food?

Firstly, alcohol usually contains refined sugar in unbelievably large quantities. The instant sugar-spike feeling is the reason most people drink in the first place. We discuss sugar addiction after this, and you will understand how being addicted to alcohol can translate into sugar addiction with its consequent implications. Because alcohol is light, the liver gives preference to its metabolism in the body. So, when you drink alcohol as part of your binge, every other digestion process goes to the backburner. This can cause severe problems, especially if you have just eaten a large amount of food. The delay in processing means that most of the food will get stored as fat deposits, causing further weight gain. When alcoholism becomes an issue, it takes precedence over every other food in the stomach and gets granted express processing. This slows down the body's metabolism. Alcohol also blocks folate absorption from the diet. Folate is a cofactor in the process of DNA synthesis. Therefore, it reduces the rate of cell repair and tissue regeneration.

In any case, alcohol is a known depressant. In fact, it is the most widely used depressant in the whole world. Does that not sound like dynamite? It is essentially bringing something that can cause depression close to a binge-eater. So, alcoholic binge-eaters go through twice the trouble. It does not help either that alcohol activates the brains' addiction and reward centers to spur you on to drink in excess. Even without any psychological disorder, alcohol can cause you to be addicted to it, and then wreak massive havoc.

To truly end your binge-eating habit, you need to cut out alcohol. You can reduce it to the barest minimum at the very least. Nobody can fight off binge-eating if they are just another alcoholic. Alcoholism and binge-eating disorder complement each other negatively.

Caffeine

Caffeine, as contained in tea and coffee, is the most widely used psychoactive drug in the world today. The chances are bright that you have already consumed a cup or two today already. However, do they contribute to binge-eating or obesity?

Actually, caffeine has no direct link to obesity or binge eating. However, caffeine is a stimulant that is often used to ward off sleep. Unfortunately, it has addictive potentials that may make it wise for you lay off it for some time until you have regained control over your eating patterns. Besides that, coffee is bitter by nature and causes people to overload on sugar and milk to neutralize the bitterness in its taste. Being overly addicted to caffeine too can cause sleep disorders bordered by anxiety. All these facilitate the chances that your mental health may be too weak to suppress any cravings that surface during that period. So, get a hand on your caffeine consumption.

I have tried to do justice to the question of what to eat to lose weight as a binge-eater. I have explained that rather than starvation or fasting to lose weight, the key is moderation and eating the right kinds of food. Now, let us talk about nutrition choices and routines that can help you maintain an optimal weight while recovering from BED.

How To Eat And Drink The Right Way

Do not starve

Starvation is the kryptonite to your attempts to destroy your binge-eating habit. Starving yourself to lose weight does nothing for your eating disorder. Rather, it worsens it and increases the chances that you will suffer a relapse very soon. Starvation prevents your body from getting what it wants at that moment. This causes a form of mental tension within you that increases with the length of the denial. At last, something snaps and you choose to indulge a little. Before you know it, you are eating up your fourth bar of chocolate.

Thus, whatever you do to lose weight, do not attempt to starve yourself. It will serve no purpose. Instead, it will just sharpen the edges of your cravings, make you more prone to break your resolve and cause you to binge in the end. With intermittent fasting, and ketogenic diets to lose weight, a binge-eater must be extremely careful. Intermittent fasting leaves a small window of time to eat, depending on the plan you adopt. However, most binge-eaters have reported that they found it hard to comply with the no-eating rule during the fasting period. As the time to break the fast approaches, they say it is harder to stay in rational control of what they put in their mouth once they can. This means the chances of losing control during the eating period is very high.

That negates the whole essence of the intermittent fasting as the calories that are shed off during the fast are recovered twofold during the eating period. Therefore, long periods of starvation are not for you if you are a binge-eater. They will only sharpen your appetite and wreck your diet weight-loss guide.

Create a meal plan for each day

BED is a full-blown disorder; there is no point denying that. As with other disorders, therefore, it needs a comprehensive plan and dedication to get defeated. We have established that starvation is not going to make it easier for one to fight BED. By that same logic, though, it is important to plan the day in terms of nutrition.

Binges sometimes occur when you are torn between many food choices and cannot pick one. Therefore, each day in the morning, you need to set out a clear meal plan detailing when you want to eat, and what you are going to eat. If you can instill self-discipline and follow your plans diligently each day, you will find out that it is easier to control your urges.

This is because since you have structured your meal times and indirectly passed a message to your subconscious self that you can only eat at those times. That greatly helps with dealing with urges and cravings.

The chances are also higher that you will choose healthier foods when you have taken time out to plan your diet instead of the haphazard logic that most people seem to consume. Therefore, it is important for you to plan your day ahead, nutrition-wise.

Do not quit cold turkey

So, you just relapsed and ate heavily again? What is the next decision? It often happens that many people take this relapse personally. They make vows not to ever binge-eat again. Or they decide to cut out a particular food form their diet. If this is not properly managed, it may end up producing an adverse effect. The goal is to reassert your control over your eating patterns gradually and not overhaul it in a single day. Quitting abruptly has a way of keeping the thought of a binge uppermost in your subconscious. You do not explore the thought, but it is there, and soon enough, it is going to be brought to the fore. Instead of quitting cold-turkey, focus on gradually reducing the amount of food you eat per binge and the frequency of the binges. The cold, hard fact is that only a microscopic few can quit binge-eating cold turkey and last more than a couple of days before relapsing. Focus on gradual reduction, not immediate cessation!

Identify your triggers

We have talked about different triggers for bingeing. These triggers play a very important role because without them; there will be no emotional eating. You need to identify the triggers that often lead you to binge-eat. It is important for you to able to figure out the most common reasons why you overeat. Could it be stress? Do you tend to overindulge yourself whenever you have a particularly tiresome day at work? Are you more likely to eat a mountain if you have a bad day at the office? Have you noticed that when you are worried about people, your primary response seems to be to open the fridge or kitchen cabinets and proceed to fill your stomach with too much food?

Everybody has specific triggers that cause them to overeat. It is important you be able to find yours. After you have found them, then you can work towards reducing the number of times that these triggers are present. It is only when you know that stress seems to push to the brink that you can take evasive measures against overeating the next time you are tired. However, if you do not know your most potent triggers, it stands to reason that you will continue to fall a victim of BED since you do not even know what causes you to overeat. Recognizing the particular triggers that cause you to overeat is an integral step in limiting their abilities to cause such reactions in you.

Practice delay

After you have decided to deal with binge-eating, there are still bound to be some relapses when you cannot control yourself. There are situations when you know that you are about to binge-eat, and you feel weak to prevent yourself from doing so. Do not beat yourself about your weakness but do not give in to your cravings just yet. Instead, try to delay yourself from eating. Speak to yourself and say, "I can wait thirty minutes surely," or something similar. Do not give in to the urge immediately. To give in is to give up control once again subconsciously. Instead, allow a little delay. Now, you may still be unable to resist the urge even after that little delay, but you would have achieved two things. Firstly, there is a subconscious agreement that you remain in charge, and secondly, you have given yourself a chance for the urge to pass. Within that little delay, something else may come up that takes your focus off food. You may find something more interesting to do and escape the upcoming episode. You may even try to fill up your belly with water or something healthy to limit the quantity of food you get to consume during the binge.

Whatever the case, do not stand up the moment you get that urge to overeat and hit the kitchen. Delay a bit, tarry a while, and you just might be able to beat the urge. Even if you don't, you have won a bit of a psychological battle that may come in handy next time you are trying to resist the urge.

Keep a food diary

Now, this advice is of a more practical nature, but it is not to be underestimated. It is perhaps the greatest device you have in your fight against overeating. You need to get yourself a small book to serve as your food diary. The book should be small enough for you to take around and fill during the day. What are you going to record in this diary? Every single thing that passes through your lips and into your throat every day. Nothing is to be left out! Not even the single cookie you accepted from your friend or the breath mint you popped into your mouth. You should try to record as soon as you finish eating. If it is not a major meal, then take out a few minutes every few hours to record what else you have eaten. That is if you cannot record it immediately.

In your diary, do not record only what you have eaten, including what you have drunk, or even licked as well. You need to make five columns in your diary for the food, the approximate quantity you ate, and the time you ate it. In the fourth column, which should be the largest, you need to record your emotions while eating.

How did you feel? Were you so eager to eat? Did you eat so very rapidly that it took you only a few minutes to polish off your entire food? How did you feel after you ate? Was there any shame or guilt? Record if you felt physical discomfort as a result of eating too much. Do not spare any details. That is why it is advised that you fill your food diary always after a major meal and even minor snacks too.

Now, title the fifth column as "reason for eating." Do not fill this column during the day or while you are eating. It is the assessment column and not to be filled immediately. Instead, at the end of each day, shortly before you go to bed, pick up your food diary and proceed to look at the entries. Read the fourth column for each and try to remember how you felt while eating that entry. Now, against each entry, write either "True hunger" or "emotional eating." Be honest with yourself; it is important. If you found out that the fourth column for a particular food item seems to say that you ate it for no reason other than the fact that you craved it, that is a sure sign that there was no hunger. Remember though, not everything we eat while not hungry qualifies as binge-eating. It is just important to keep an eye on them so that you can see just how frequently you consume a particular item.

Keep your food diary, religiously. Each night, go through it and reflect on how many binge episodes you had that day. Think of how you can prevent such next time. In essence, the food diary is a sort of research tool for you to check your eating habit and determine how well you are dealing with BED. It will also help you know what your triggers are, and the impulses that push you to overeat. Besides, it can serve to help you compare your meal plan each day with what you actually ate.

The food diary is a key component of dealing with binge-eating. Knowing that everything you eat is going to get recorded and accounted for can even give you a psychological edge that can help fight acute cravings.

To end this chapter, let me make a concluding statement. Weight loss therapy is perhaps the most effective therapy for binge-eating. What we eat and how we eat is going to play a key role in fighting off binge-eating. Its eradication itself is a gradual process premised on accountability and eating right. There is no point starving yourself to lose weight as a binge-eater. It may work for others, but you are sufficiently addicted to ensure that starvation will only raise the desire to binge even higher. A food diary is both a psychological and physical device that can help you monitor your addiction, as well as how effective your attempts to cure it have been. In conclusion, for a binge-eater, the idea of weight loss therapy is first to institute a balanced diet tilted towards helping to get rid of the food addiction. If and when BED is gotten rid of, then attention can be shifted to actual, proper weight loss.

Chapter 8

SUGAR ADDICTION AND BINGE EATING

❖❖❖❖❖❖❖❖❖❖❖❖❖❖❖❖

It is everywhere around us, in the food we eat and the drinks we consume. Its soul-warming, soft feel on the tongue is perhaps the most recognizable and distinctive of tastes. Everyone loves the taste of sugar but is it exactly the healthiest thing to take, especially for a recovering or active binge-eater? That is the question to answer in this chapter.

Let me start by quickly clearing up a misconception. Sugar does not just refer to the white, granulated stuff we put in our tea and coffee to sweeten them. Instead, sugar exists in so many numerous forms that it becomes impossible to track unless you know what you are after. Even in the foods, you will least expect, such as fruits and vegetables, some sugar exists. That sugar is present in a lot of food is not the issue at hand here, though. It is the fact that you can get addicted to sugar? Do you have doubts?

In much the same way as BED is about food addiction, sugar addiction is a real health threat. It may be silent, but it is no less a threat any day. I favor the statistics as usual. So, let us look at some.

The American Heart Association estimates that sugar intake for a woman should not exceed a hundred calories daily, while a man's intake should be below 155 calories. Here is breaking news for you. The average American consumes an approximate 355 calories of sugar each day. That represents over three hundred percent increase compared to the dietary guidelines. The most dangerous part of sugar addiction, though, is that most people are not even aware they are addicted.

The thing with sugar is that it is everywhere in our diet. So, there is no escaping it. Therefore, when one becomes addicted to it, it is very easy to facilitate and satisfy this addiction. It is also somewhat hard to get weaned off an addiction to something you must continue to feed upon.

Sugar in our diet exists either as simple sugar or complex sugar. Simple sugars, as found in table sugar, are referred to as monosaccharide. A monosaccharide is the smallest unit of sugar in existence. They are of different forms such as glucose and fructose; they also combine to form more complex sugars known as oligosaccharides and polysaccharides. Sugar is contained in a wide variety of carbohydrates, fruits, and vegetables. Upon consuming a sugar-containing food, digestion starts with amylase, an enzyme found in saliva. After digestion, sugar gets broken down into glucose, which insulin then proceeds to move into the cells that need it for energy production. However, insulin also moves certain other proteins alongside sugar into the cells; this leaves a compound, tryptophan, free and circulating in the bloodstream.

This tryptophan plays a vital role in the development of sugar addiction. It activates a complex known as the mesolimbic system in the brain. This system is responsible for the production of dopamine, one of the happiness hormones. Dopamine further activates a center in the brain known as the *nucleus accumbens*. This is the center responsible for the control, regulation, and activation of addictions and cravings in the human brain. This entire sequence of events serves to produce a pleasant feeling all over the body that ensures that the body will be back yearning for more sugar before long.

In combination with the naturally sweet taste of sugar, the dopamine release causes an addiction to sugary food that is very hard to throw off. How does all this tie in with BED?

Sugar addiction is one of the principal components of binge-eating. It is safe to say that almost all binge-eaters have some form of sugar dependence or the other. It is a significant cornerstone in emotional eating. It is practically impossible to consume as much food as a typical binge-eater, and not develop some dependence on sugar. It may come as maltose, refined sugar, brown sugar, fructose or corn syrup, but sugar, in any form, has a real potential for addiction.

Each one of your binge episodes, when you reach out for that soda bottle, you are not just reacting to emotions, there is a real chance that you are being prompted by sugar addiction as well. Sugar addiction follows a similar path as The Binge Cycle. In sugar addiction, there are three primary stages;

- The feasting,

- Withdrawal, and

- Craving stages.

The feasting stage, which often coincides with the bingeing phase in The Binge Cycle, involves consuming sugary foods in excess along with other classes of food. After the initial glucose high caused by the ingestion of sugar, the sharp decrease in blood sugar causes symptoms of sugar withdrawal, which may include mood changes, anxiety, irritability, and fatigue. This then leads to the craving stage, which plays out in the same way as in The Binge Cycle. Things are pretty much complicated by the fact that the body gradually develops sugar tolerance. It takes progressively increasing amounts of sugar to keep you satisfied as your body continues to adjust to the amount you regularly take. So, you may find yourself taking two cans of soft drinks after meals instead of the single can you are used to.

Now, what factors promote the development of sugar addiction or its excessive consumption?

Starvation

Our body is wired to seek for survival at all times. So, when you get starved, the brain works even harder than usual to not only inform you of the need for more glucose but also devotes a large part of its function to seek out food. Too often, unfortunately, the object of desire is sugar-laden food that can provide an immediate supply of energy for the body to continue its normal functions. If this gets repeated too often, you may rewire your addiction center to crave for sugar as the instant fix whenever you are hungry, tired, or in emotional upheaval. This causes the addiction to grow.

Stress

Stressful states are often characterized by a need for energy supplementation. In the confusion and fatigue that often trail stress, many people wrongly turn towards sugar to restore some balance and equilibrium. This may become a habit quite quickly. So, each time they get stressed out, their brain tells them to refuel with the *sugariest* thing, they can lay their hands upon.

Processed foods

So important is processed food to the entire concept of BED that it gets its chapter right after this. Processed foods are often packed full of sugar to improve their taste. Their ready availability also means that they are often the first choice of food for a lot of people. What happens when your first choice of food is very high in sugar? Sugar addiction most likely.

Habit

Let's forget the biology for a moment. You don't even need it to get addicted to something with as great a taste as sugar has. So, sugar addiction can quite literally arise from a genuine love of the taste. Many people love chocolates for the taste, just as many would do anything to lay hands on a bowl of ice-cream before retiring to bed. Therefore, seeking the taste of sugar in its various guises can become a habit that pretty much leads to addiction to it.

There are other reasons why sugar addiction might arise but let us stop at these major ones. From my explanation above, it is pretty clear that it is almost impossible to get rid of emotional eating if you do not take care of any underlying sugar addiction. That is one of the reasons why people fail to get rid of binge-eating disorder. There can be no end in sight for your BED if you do not root out your sugar addiction.

Apart from sponsoring binge-eating even, an addiction to sugar poses other immediate and delayed threats to your overall wellbeing. For instance, sugar addiction means that you may end up overloading on calories and gain unneeded weight in due course. That comes with issues we have discussed extensively in previous chapters. Tooth decay is another feature of poor health that may develop if your diet is high in sugar content.

Especially during a feasting phase, hyperactivity owing to the very high levels of blood glucose has been reported. Naturally, there is also an increased chance of diabetes mellitus. In a normal, physically active individual, excess sugar should be dealt with quite effectively. However, research has shown that consistently high levels of blood sugar and a reduction in the ability of cells to sense insulin is related. There are also psychosomatic effects of sugar addiction. Withdrawal and cravings for sugar can trigger less-than-desirable signs such as fatigue, restlessness, parched throats, and general discomfort.

So, how can you stop sugar-addiction? Stopping sugar-addiction needs to follow the same course as trying to get rid of binge-eating.

Most of the methods discussed in part three apply to both disorders. However, here are some tips specifically applicable to sugar addiction.

- *A Balanced nutrition*

From the moment you realize you have a sugar addiction; it is important to switch over to a balanced diet that contains all the different classes of food in better proportion. Diets high in carbohydrates have often be fingered as propagating sugar-addiction. So, you need to look over your nutrition and reduce the amount of starchy food that you get to consume daily. That will help lower your tolerance threshold for sugar and give you a medium to gradually reduce the amount of sugar you get daily.

- *Substitute soft drinks for water or tea.*

Soft drinks, including soda, are some of the handiest, most straightforward ways to gulp tons after tons of sugar into your body system. They offer a refreshing feeling and give you an almost instant boost of energy, but that is not enough reason to remain addicted to sugar. Instead, the next time you feel like taking a drink, think water or tea in place of fizzy drinks.

- *Consume plenty of water*

Water performs so many functions in the body. We are going to get to them later. To fight off sugar-addiction though, you can consume a lot of water to induce satiety and limit the amount of sugar that you need to consume. Think of it this way. Each time you get a craving, first gulp down a glass or two of water. That way, even if you still get to consume the sugary food, it is likely it will be in smaller quantities as water has already filled a substantial part of your stomach space. Water also rehydrates the body when you are under stress or fatigued. Drinking enough water can preclude the need to consume more sugar.

- *Swap starch for protein and fiber*

Starchy foods like tubers contain very high glucose content that causes a sugar spike when eaten. Since the idea of recovery from sugar addiction is to limit the amount of sugar in the diet, it is prudent to swap such starchy food for better options. Heavy starch can be replaced with proteinous options such as nuts, and fiber through fruits and vegetables.

- *Regular exercise*

This is a management tip rather than advice on how to be rid of sugar addiction. If you are addicted already, the worst thing you can do is live a sedentary lifestyle devoid of any meaningful physical activity. That is an express ticket to feeling all the side effects of your addiction. Instead, burning off the excess sugar can be a crucial decider in your favor. Rigorous exercise can at least mean that you are getting out the sugar you are putting in your body system.

- *Empty your house of sugar*

I do not think I need to tell you this. Out of sight is out of mind in this case. I do not advise you to quit abruptly because that usually fails nine out of ten times. However, you cannot eat what you do not have. Your battle against sugar addiction should start from your choices at the grocery stores and what you stack on your kitchen shelves. You should get rid of the obvious options such as refined table sugar, carbonated drinks, and jam, for some time at least. You are bound to escape some few cravings for sugar if you do not have it staring at you from every corner of your kitchen.

- *Do not switch to sweeteners*

Switching from sugar to artificial replacements and sweeteners is a fool's errand, so to speak. It is like cladding sugar in other robes and pretending it isn't the one. Aspartame and saccharine, for instance, are nothing but sugar in another form and called by another name. So, when and if you change sugar to artificial sweeteners, you are merely exchanging one dagger for another.

- *Join a detox program*

Addictions often require external support to be fought off. Joining a sugar detox program, therefore, will avail you of professional help and excellent advice on how to beat your sugar addiction.

To end this chapter, let me reiterate this;

> **"There is no defeating binge-eating if you suffer from sugar addiction."**

Sugar addiction is BED's trusted lieutenant. You cannot get rid of one when the other is present. Therefore, one must make the ultimate commitment to end sugar addiction if one is to fob binge-eating away successfully.

Chapter 9

THE SCOURGE THAT IS PROCESSED FOODS

If sugar addiction is a vital, integral part of binge-eating, then excessive consumption of processed food has been the conduit that has supplied the vast majority of the addictive potentials of food these days. As a specie, human food has changed drastically over the last few centuries. For instance, Ancient Man fed on small animals he could hunt initially, then discovered that he could eat little shrubs and plants as well. From that moment up until about a hundred and twenty years ago, the diet of the average man featured mostly natural, and fresh food items. At the turn of the twentieth century, meals still mainly consisted of animal and plant products that had undergone very minimal chemical processing. All that has changed now, though.

A cursory look at the menu in most restaurants now show a wide variety of food items that would have sounded very strange only a century ago. This is because we have gradually shifted from natural food towards processed food items, and we are none the better for the change. That explains why we have more cases of diet-related diseases and conditions today, such as diabetes and hypertension.

Processed foods are also culpable in the progression and sustainment of a binge-eating disorder. How so? First, let me define processed foods. Processed foods in this context refer to any food that has undergone processing (mainly chemical) before being sold onto consumers. This processing is often done to preserve this food for longer, improve their taste, or introduce a unique flavor. Simple, mechanical processing such as drying, grilling, or milling does not count as processing here.

When you look at my definition, it suddenly becomes clear that the most substantial part of what the average man eats today is processed food. Virtually ninety-five percent of what you see on the shelves in the mall is processed food. Soft drinks, chocolate, oils, cookies, sweets, your favorite ice-cream, and cornflakes are all processed foods designed to last for longer. But at what cost?

While the desire to extend the shelf-life of food items may have been commendable, the potential ill-effects that processing causes far outweighs the potential benefits. In any case, extending the shelf lives is an adjunct reason rather than the primary reason. The truth, in fact, is that the food industry is a highly competitive world with each manufacturer having to compete with many dozen other manufacturers with similar products.

The drive to succeed led most manufacturers on a journey to discover just how they may acquire a larger share of their market. So, each started experimenting with their products to make them more appealing to consumers. The result is that a lot of what we have on our shelves today have been designed to keep us addicted to them. The average processed food now is loaded with enough sugar and a particular taste to keep you glued to it. The side effect of this aggressive drive for more customers has led to products which may pass dietary guidelines laid down by regulatory agencies but actually, pose subtle threats.

Show me a man addicted to processed foods, and you have yourself a binge-eater most likely. The truth, though, is that most people depend on these processed foods to get along each day. Sadly, the constituents of these processed foods make it almost impossible for you not to become attached. That is bad news for binge-eating disorder.

I ask you to cast your mind back to your last binge. What foods did you feast upon? I bet the larger majority was processed foods rather than natural options. It is much more common to find people addicted to carbonated drinks and coffee, for instance than fresh fruit juice. A list of the most common foods that people get addicted to will certainly feature options such as chocolate, ice-cream, cookies, fizzy drinks, alcohol, etc. before you find tubers or unprocessed, whole grains.

What does all this mean for your fight against binge-eating disorder? This simply means that it is going to be a tough ask for you to beat binge-eating disorder without cutting down on the percentage of processed foods you consume each day. Take a look at your food diary, if you have already started one and look at just how much processed foods you eat daily and you will understand the significance that these foods have in BED. In fact, they facilitate the disorder itself.

Unfortunately, one of the primary lures of processed foods is that they are around us everywhere, readily available, and cheap even. They come in easy-to-prepare modes, and that makes them more attractive to the average consumer. Just consider how easy it is to make a cup of tea or eat some cornflakes, and you will understand why and how processed foods gained so much ground. Compare the ease with making fresh fruit juice from the beginning.

Matters are not helped by the fact that processed foods are available in virtually every variety you can think of; as solids, liquids, or even semi-cooked packages. There are even different flavors for different foods. The marketing is also so overwhelming that it is hard not to get fixated on these foods. Unfortunately, processed foods aren't really the greatest options for our tables.

If you are serious about getting rid of emotional eating, cutting out processed foods to the barest minimum is a basic requirement. Why do I say so? Let us take a look at just some of the reasons why you should not consume processed foods too much.

An Abundance of preservatives

If I asked anyone out on the streets if they would like to consume a spoon of nitrosamine or E160, chances are I would get very few takers. This would not be because they hadn't heard of nitrosamine before but because the name sounds chemical enough for them not to want in their systems. Yet, nitrosamine is just one of those chemicals we consume each time we plop into the mall and grab that jar or that packet. Under the guise of preservatives, manufacturers force us all to consume so many different chemicals of different origins that it is a wonder that we do not notice. Pick up a packet of your favorite cookies, or a jar of mayonnaise and read the ingredients label. Now, tell me just how many of the entries you found present sounded like real food that you will like to have.

Sadly, the reality is that we keep consuming these preservatives, most of which when they build up in the body over time, become toxic and can potentially serve as harbingers of a whole lot of health problems. In this regard, binge-eating is the least of your worries. Not only are most of the ingredients and preservatives foreign to our body system, but the manufacturers are also not even compelled to disclose the full contents of their products. You may find something such as "artificial flavoring" as an ingredient without any elucidation as to what it is made of. These are termed trade secrets that each manufacturer needs to preserve as his own. So, the average individual continues to be fed a recipe made up in part of artificial chemicals and unknown substances. If that is not scary enough, I wonder what is.

Excess sugar and salt

The competition out in the food industry is very fierce. Each manufacturer wants a larger market share. So, they all try to target the brain's addiction center at all times to keep you hooked. That is why you prefer a particular brand of chocolate to others. To do this, they utilize the most effective weapon at their disposal; sugar. Like

I told you in the previous chapter, sugar addiction is real and is one tough addiction to shake off.

Therefore, most processed foods are loaded with sugar under various names. The excessive sugar content ensures that you acquire a loyalty to that particular food and remain a consistent consumer. In this regard, perhaps nothing is worse than soft drinks. A cursory look at even Youtube will reveal videos of researches that show the startling amount of sugar in the more common brands like Pepsi and Coca-cola. As if that was not enough, a lot of these foods also contain way too much salt. That gives them their spicy taste, alongside seasoning. The excess sodium from this salt causes an imbalance in electrolyte levels.

Immediate sugar boost

Processed foods consist of refined sugars in high quantity. This sugar does not need to be digested before it is even absorbed. It goes straight into the bloodstream to cause an immediate sugar spike. We have already discussed the significance of this in binge-eating disorder. With time, you run the risk of developing insulin insensitivity when you keep consuming processed foods in large quantities.

Highly addictive

A lot of thoughts, ideas, and processes go into manufacturers' attempts to boost sales and retain more customers. The average processed foods maker is trying his best to make his products look as enticing as possible to get you hooked on them. So, it is no surprise that a lot of people have *favorite* ice-cream flavors, cookies, or juice. The addictive potentials of processed foods mean that you are likely to feast on them regularly. That increases the risk you have, of developing binge-eating.

High calories value

Processed foods are often high in empty, useless calories which do not serve much of a physiological use. Instead, they disbalance your calories equation, resulting in an unnecessary increase in your calorie intake without a corresponding compensation in expenditure. Therefore, your body needs to work harder if it is to burn these calories. This does you no favor if you are trying to lose weight.

Not made for you

Let us be frank. The processed foods industry is not a consumer-oriented one. Rather, it is driven by profit margins and capturing new consumers. Therefore, do not expect that any decision that will not try to get you even more addicted is about to be passed. Instead, the newest products on the line are tailored even to get you more addicted and unable to resist the temptations that come with eating them.

Processed foods are detrimental to anyone's health, not just patients suffering from BED. They are high in sugar, sodium, and trans fats, which are not healthy enough for you. To compound issues, they have high addictive tendencies, which means that you are more likely to use them as a base ingredient for your binges. If you are looking to avoid or get rid of binge eating disorder, then you can do worse than listen to Michael Pollan's advice. He said; "If it came from a plant, eat it. If it was made in a plant, don't eat it". Processed foods are not the safest food option that a binge-eater can go in for. Rather, they greatly increase the chance that you will become addicted to food and go on a binge.

Chapter 10

COGNITIVE BEHAVIORAL THERAPY

Cognitive behavioral therapy (CBT) is a modality of psychological therapy that is aimed at assessing patients' thought patterns and how these affect their actions and behaviors. It is typically employed in the treatment of psychosocial anomalies, such as certain phobias, addictions, depression, anxiety, and dietary disorders. In essence, CBT makes patients solve their mental problems by encouraging them to challenge their negative, harmful thoughts, habits, and behaviors. CBT is essentially a short-term treatment method with a working principle that a person's thoughts, emotions, and actions are all interwoven and, therefore, affect one another. By focusing on and modifying negative thought, one can change their emotional response to a stimulus, and thus alter their course of action, which ultimately leads to a shift in behavioral pattern. This thought-emotion-action cycle is central to the effectiveness of CBT in treating disorders.

CBT is more or less a guiding hand, which directs people to believe they can and strive to solve their distress. According to the American Psychological Association, a patient undergoing cognitive behavioral therapy soon learns to see themselves as their therapist. CBT is a highly structured, problem-specific therapy with a limited number of one-on-one sessions between the patient and therapist, focused on quickly identifying the causative factors of a disorder and providing short-term solutions to it. Its effectiveness and low demands as regards time are two of the factors that have made it the most common and sought after type of therapy. It has been proven to be efficacious in the treatment of Post-traumatic stress disorder (PTSD), sleep disorders, anxiety, depression, binge-eating disorder, obsessive-compulsive disorder, sexual disorders, and bipolar disorders. Solely, or in conjunction with other forms of therapy, CBT can:

- Help a patient cope with symptoms of a psychiatric ailment

- Prevent symptoms of mental ailment from recurring

- Be a good alternative to drugs, especially when a drug is contraindicated for use, or when a patient is allergic to a prescribed drug

- Teach you methods and strategies to manage stressful or complicated situations or circumstances

- Assist patients in keeping emotions in check

- Help deal with psychological and emotional trauma taking roots in violent or abusive experiences

- Help alleviate pain from chronic diseases, according to new studies

CBT is usually undertaken in treatment courses, each of which is broken down into several sessions. There are usually 20 sessions in a CBT course, though this is not consistent throughout all CBT treatment regimens. CBT can teach patients to:

- Assess and understand problems more vividly and objectively
- Be aware of the inception of negative thoughts
- Challenge self-made conclusions and core beliefs that may not be true
- Draw a line between hard facts and illogical thoughts
- Have an understanding of the way past events and experiences can shape the present reality
- Eliminate their fear of worst-case scenarios
- Develop more than one viewpoint of assessing a situation
- Know why people do what they do, and to understand their convictions
- Be more positive and optimistic while scrutinizing their circumstances

- Be more sensitive to mood changes

- Create achievable goals

- Blame themselves less for unfavorable happenings

- Tune into reality rather than lingering in their fantasies of how things should be

- Be bold enough to confront their fears rather than trying to escape them

- Be less judgmental and critical of themselves and others

Cognitive behavioral therapy encourages patients first to identify, then challenge unreasonable, illogical, or harmful thoughts, and finally develop skills to fight off these thoughts. Though this form of talk therapy is used in many other types of psychological and psychiatric treatment, CBT has risen as the most commonly used of all. CBT is also considered by many as the most effective type of talk therapy, especially for patients who are willing to inculcate treatment strategies into their lives. CBT often requires fewer sessions per course, compared to other therapies, and although it might require continuous participation of patients over long periods, it is still regarded by many patients as the best technique of mental healing. Also, being a short-term therapy, CBT is usually cheaper than other therapies; this is another reason why it is the most desirable. In the face of the seemingly innumerable advantages and applications of CBT, it does, however, come with a few glitches. Some of these are:

- Cognitive behavioral therapy is overly depended on the cooperation of the patient. The therapist or counselor can talk to the patient and help analyze their problems, but it ultimately depends on the patient to decide if they want to heal.

- CBT needs full commitment from the patient to deliver optimum results

- CBT usually prescribes strategies – which the patient would have to incorporate into their life –, and homework to be carried out by the patient; this can take up a lot of the patient's time.

- CBT is highly structured and organized; hence, it may not be an appropriate means of treatment for individuals who have complicated mental or intellectual issues, such as people who have learning or speech difficulties.

- CBT requires lots of courage and stability, as it digs out one's emotions and fears. The sessions can be emotionally distressing.

- CBT aims at encouraging patients to change themselves by modifying their thoughts and emotions – this method of therapy does not give room for other factors outside of a patient's control that can affect the patient's mental wellbeing, such as family background and childhood experiences. The concept of CBT is not wide enough to consider the root causes of mental ailments, as it focuses on solving current problems.

One of the central focusing points of CBT is the automatic negative thoughts that can creep effortlessly into the mind and either induce or worsen mental disorders, such as anxiety and depression. These automatic thoughts sprout at will, are considered true and have a predilection for negatively affecting an individual's mood. During a CBT course, patients are encouraged to bring these thoughts to the surface, assess them based on evidence from reality, and judge whether they hold true or not. By so doing, patients can have a more objective evaluation of the thought patterns that cause or contribute to their mental illnesses, and, therefore, develop healthier ones.

CBT utilizes various techniques to accomplish psychotherapy. They include:

- **Rational Emotive Behavior Therapy (REBT):** REBT is a type of cognitive behavioral therapy that is aimed at identifying, challenging, and modifying patients' illogical and unreasonable beliefs.

- **Cognitive Therapy:** This form of CBT is focused on identifying and altering false thoughts and deformed emotions and behavioral patterns.

- **Multimodal Therapy:** This type of CBT is centered on treating mental ailments through the understanding of seven independent but intertwined factors, namely behavior, affect, sensation, imagery, cognition, interpersonal factors and drug/biological factors.

- **Dialectical Behavior Therapy:** This CBT modality addresses distortions in patients' thought and behavioral patterns by employing techniques such as mindfulness and emotional control.

Cognitive Behavioral Therapy in Treating BED

Binge eating disorder is a complicated mental abnormality, which impacts negatively on the brain and body. It is thought that negative shouts, emotions, and actions can induce binge eating. Overeating has the potential to cause serious health problems, such as obesity and certain diseases. Since binge eating starts as a problem of the mind, it is logical to try to correct it by first addressing the mind. This is where cognitive behavioral therapy come in. The primary goal of CBT is to help binge eaters identify the negative thought and behavior patterns that cause them to overeat and then formulate strategies for developing more positive ones.

CBT is the foremost evidence-based method for treating persons with binge eating disorder. It is adequate for treating children, adolescents, and adults, and emphasized the roles that both cognitive and behavioral factors play in the exacerbation and alleviation of eating disorders. Cognitive factors that play a part in binge eating disorder include over-assessment of body weight and physique, negative self-image, distorted beliefs about self-esteem, perfectionist thoughts, and distorted self-evaluation. Some behavioral factors that influence binge eating are restricting oneself from eating, self-harm, purging, and avoidance of body checking.

People suffering from binge eating disorder typically have a false sense and belief of themselves and their physiques. They often inhabit critical reviews of themselves, which can lead to feelings of disgust or shame. These unhealthy feelings create a vicious cycle of weight control behaviors and negative self-assessment. The role of a CBT practitioner is to assist the patient in ascertaining the specific set of factors that contribute to their binge eating behaviors and developing goals geared towards nullifying their bingeing behaviors.

Cognitive behavioral therapy has three phases of treatment, all of which emphasize and implement training regimens aimed at providing the patients with an understanding of themselves and their bingeing. Only through an in-depth understanding of self and the disorder can any sort of healing occur. The phases of treatment involved in CBT are the behavioral phase, cognitive phase, and maintenance and relapse prevention phase.

The Behavioral Phase

In this phase, the patient and counselor/therapist develop rapport and then collaborate to develop a plan to normalize dietary behaviors and eliminate bingeing symptoms. This is the stage where emotions are usually at their peak; therefore, it is imperative to create tools and strategies for coping with the emotions that may gush forth. The activities that take place during this phase of the therapy include:

- Identifying and alleviating negative behaviors attached to binge eating disorder, and behaviors developed by the patient as a result of the disgust, shame, or guilt brought upon by bingeing.

- Educating the patient on a balanced diet, proper times to eat, and required nutrients.

- They are creating tools and strategies for handling emotions that may lead to binge eating. Patients are taught the acts of distraction, urge prolonging, and stoppage of thoughts as strategies for overcoming their binge eating behaviors.

The Cognitive Phase

In the cognitive phase, the negative thought patterns associated with binge eating are identified, and the first attempts to challenge and modify them are made. The techniques used to achieve this are called cognitive restructuring techniques, which, in collaboration with the patient, the therapist can use to alter the causative and to exacerbate thoughts of binge eating. For instance, say a patient who is on CBT for binge eating has started on a healthy dietary regimen to help get them off bingeing. The patient gets home one day, while in the course of healing and 'accidentally' eats a chocolate cookie. As a binge eater, the primary thoughts the patient would have (the automatic thoughts) would be along the lines of thinking that as a result of eating that one chocolate cookie, they are going to gain weight, or the therapy had been made null and void. These thoughts can make the patient give up on the therapy and revert to binge eating, as they think all hope of recovery is now lost. Consequently, the patient feels guilty, depressed, and anxious, and thus take dietary restriction measures, followed by episodes of binge eating. This leads to further depression, anxiety, and guilt; and the cycle continues.

In the cognitive phase of CBT, the fictitious patient above would be encouraged to identify and air those unhealthy thoughts that worsen their binge eating. Afterward, they are taught to evaluate these thoughts in light of pieces of evidence that either support or refute them. There is no evidence, scientific or otherwise, that supports the thought that eating one chocolate cookie can lead to weight gain; on the other hand, there are tons of scientific evidence that oppose it the notion that eating one bar of chocolate cookie can cause one to gain weight. Hence, the thought is considered illogical, irrational, and untrue, and should, therefore, be abandoned. Then, the patient is encouraged to develop new, positive thoughts, for example, "eating a bar of chocolate cookie will not make me fat, so, it is better for me not to binge-eat and revert to my old ways, as that is unhealthy for me. Though I made the mistake of eating a chocolate cookie which is not part of my dietary regimen, I will stick to the plan and see it through. This is better for me and my health." As a result of the modification of the thought process, the patient feels less depressed, less anxious, and higher self-esteem, and develops a feeling of achievement.

The activities that generally take place during the cognitive phase of treatment include:

- Overcoming negative and unhealthy thoughts about self and self-worth, as well as eliminating the need to be perfect as it is usually unrealistic and farfetched.

- The therapist helps the patient to assess the implications and impact of negative thoughts about themselves on their relationships with others. The patient is then taught to develop interpersonal and communication skills.

- The patient is advised to be more optimistic and positive about themselves and their health.

The Maintenance and Relapse Prevention Phase

The final phase of a CBT course is the maintenance and relapse prevention phase. In this phase, the patient is encouraged to maintain and focus on the skills and strategies learned in the prior phases. The patient creates a relapse prevention plan in collaboration with the therapist, to help them stick to the treatment plan and combat remnant and new negative thoughts and behaviors. The activities in this phase include:

- Building self-confidence in the patient through the repeated application, by the patient, of learned skills.

- Identifying cues that bring about negative thoughts and dealing with them appropriately.

- Assessing the level of progress made thus far by the patient in the course of therapy.

- Attaining complete healing and the disappearance of binge eating symptoms, hence completing the treatment plan.

Scientific Assessment of the Efficacy of CBT for the Treatment of BED

Scientific research has proven the efficacy of cognitive behavioral therapy in the treatment of binge eating disorder. Some studies that infer the effectiveness of CBT in treating bingeing are highlighted as follows:

- A study published by the Journal of Eating Disorders in 2006 concluded that cognitive behavioral therapy was the more efficacious treatment for binge eating, as compared with behavioral weight loss therapy (BWLT). The study involved eighty participants diagnosed with binge eating disorder who were randomly assigned to two groups, with one group treated with CBT and the other with BWLT. The treatments lasted a total of sixteen weeks. Although this superior effectiveness was achieved in the short-term, it was more difficult to see a difference in the efficacies of both treatment methods in the long run.

- The *Behavior Therapy* journal published a study in 1993, which compared the efficacies of CBT, weight loss treatment, and desipramine in the treatment of binge eating disorder. The study involved 108 obese participants with binge eating disorder who were randomly distributed to three groups – one group received CBT, then second was treated with desipramine, and the third received weight loss therapy. After three months of treatment, the group receiving CBT had achieved more reduction in the symptoms of binge eating disorder than any of the other two groups.

- In 2002, Wilfley *et al.* published a study in which 162 participants diagnosed with binge eating disorder were randomly distributed into two groups, one receiving CBT and the other Interpersonal Psychotherapy (IPT). The study concluded that after 20 weeks of treatment sessions, both CBT and IPT had significantly reduced binge eating disorder symptoms in the participants.

- Grilo *et all* published research in the journal *Biological Psychiatry* in 2005. It included 108 participants with binge eating disorder who were randomly assigned to four groups; one treated with CBT and placebo, the second with fluoxetine, the third with a combination of CBT and fluoxetine, and the fourth with placebo alone. After sixteen weeks of treatment, the study concluded that CBT, not fluoxetine, was effective in the treatment of binge eating disorder.

- A 2015 study published in the *Behavior Research and Therapy* journal concluded that CBT is an effective treatment of individuals with an eating disorder, after one hundred and thirty participants with various eating disorders were treated for twenty weeks.

Alongside weight loss, Cognitive behavioral therapy remains the best treatment method available to people with binge eating disorder. It provides a structured, evidence-based pathway for decreasing and even eliminating symptoms of binge eating, through multiphase therapy courses consisting of balanced, high-yield sessions. CBT can be employed as a standalone treatment method, or in conjunction with other treatment methods to rid patients of bingeing symptoms and return them to normal dieting.

Chapter 11

OTHER THERAPIES FOR BINGE EATING DISORDER

Aside from weight loss therapy and cognitive behavioral therapy, other approaches to BED are discussed in this chapter.

Dialectical Behavior Therapy (DBT)

Dialectical behavior therapy is a modality of treating people suffering from mental ailments, including binge eating disorder. Essentially, DBT is a type of cognitive behavioral therapy focused on assisting people in attaining and living a life free from mental suffering.

It was originally designed in the late 1980s by Dr. Marsha Linehan as a therapeutic measure for persons who practice self-harm, many of whom also suffer from 'borderline personality disorder.' DBT is a treatment method that incorporates treatment techniques of the east with those of the western countries, such as cognitive behavioral therapy.

The eastern techniques incorporated into DBT account for the psychological and spiritual practices. This include mindfulness, which teaches people to accept circumstances rather than attempt to change them, and to control complicated emotions. On the flip side, Dialectical behavioral therapy has often come under attack by critics who state that it does don't pay attention to emotional dysregulation, a condition characterized with difficulty in exhibiting emotional responses that are considered culturally acceptable.

In addition to binge eating disorder, the concepts of DBT have also proven effective in the treatment of mood disorders, suicidal predilection, post-traumatic stress disorder (PTSD), alcohol problems, depression, traumatic brain injury (TBI), and substance abuse. It helps people to get more control over their emotions and thoughts by identifying the triggers that induce distressful emotional responses, as well as develop skills to manage thoughts, emotions, behaviors, and events that may lead to undesirable actions.

DBT usually comprises treatment sessions tailored towards meeting each patient's unique situation, as well as sessions for skills groups. In the individual sessions, the patient comes in contact directly with a therapist or counselor who assesses the patient's unique circumstances and then formulates treatment plans. The therapist also has to ensure that patients remain motivated throughout the therapy course, that they incorporate learned skillset into their daily lives, and that they are encouraged to examine the factors that may impede their healing process.

DBT is made up of four modules, namely Mindfulness, Distress Tolerance, Emotion Regulation, and Interpersonal Effectiveness.

Mindfulness

Mindfulness is the central point of all DBT concepts. It is the art of mastering one's mind rather than allowing it to be in control, which translates into the ability to focus attention on the present moment in an objective, non-judgmental way. The concept of mindfulness comprises meditations derived from Buddhism, although the practice does not include any form of religious supernatural acts. Mindfulness teaches people to exist at the moment and accept and enjoy one's emotions to the fullest. It makes people aware of the powers of the senses and encourages their optimum use toward understanding the environment. Mindfulness depends significantly on an individual's capacity to accept circumstances and situations without questioning or passing judgment and to accept the emotional reactions that arise in response to situations, as well as their causative situations. When people learn to accept things this way, they are apt to become less distressed and less uncomfortable. The mindfulness module helps people to:

- Be more sensitive to information originating from within themselves, information that they would not have been aware of

- Have a firmer grip on their thoughts, emotions, and responses

- Be able to move attention away from an unhelpful thought or situation to a more beneficial one.

Distress Tolerance

As its name implies, distress tolerance is the ability to tolerate and accept emotional distress or suffering. Accepting distress is key to a state of sound mental health since distress is part of life and cannot be avoided or eliminated. Mastering distress tolerance is vital in the treatment of binge eating since binge eaters usually binge to relieve stress or pain. Without the ability to endure pain and distress, people would usually revert to their old ways, as the process of recovering from bingeing is not a particularly easy one. The essence of the distress tolerance module lies in eliminating or at least reducing impulsive behaviors, such as binge eating, and replace them with healthier ways of dealing with distress, such as self-soothing, distraction, and IMPROVE techniques.

Self-soothing, as used in DBT, is a technique in which people are encouraged to act in a soothing, mild, and soft way to oneself. It is typically used in distressing or painful moments to manage negative thoughts and find relief.

Distraction helps individuals to distract themselves from undesirable emotions for a while by using the ACCEPTS method as described below:

Activities: Individuals can employ useful activities they enjoy doing.

Contribute: Individuals may reach out to people within their community to help them out.

Comparisons: Comparisons should be drawn between oneself and a less fortunate person, or between one's current state and a time when one was in a worse condition.

Emotions: Individuals should trigger positive emotions in themselves, for example, by cracking a joke or reading a hilarious paragraph in a book.

Push away: individuals are encouraged to attempt to push the present undesirable situation aside and replace it temporarily with a more pleasant one.

Thoughts: One should force themselves to think of other things.

Sensations: It is recommended to engage in something that triggers an intense feeling, such as taking a cold shower.

The IMPROVE technique is a skill used to assist people in relieving stress during moments of distress. It goes as thus:

- **I**magery: Use mental imagery to visualize relaxing scenarios, such as beaches, gardens, and 'smiling cats.'

- **M**eaning: Seek meaning in the way you are feeling at the moment.

- **P**rayer: Say some personal prayers or recite mantras.

- **R**elaxation: In conjunction with self-soothing, relax your muscles and use relaxation breathing techniques.

- **O**ne thing in the moment: Identify what you are doing at the moment and try to direct all of your energy towards it.

- **V**acation: Give yourself a short break from everything.

- **E**ncouragement: Motivate and encourage yourself to handle the present situation.

Emotion Regulation

As earlier mentioned, people with binge eating disorder sometimes binge to dull painful or distressing emotions. Therefore, there is a need for these people to be able to control or regulate their emotions, as doing that would help them recover better and quicker. Emotion regulation in DBT focuses on:

- Identifying, assessing, and validating one's emotions.

- Increasing the patient's resilience to negative emotions and increasing positive emotions.

- Teaching patients to let go of distressful emotions voluntarily.

Interpersonal Effectiveness

Having a good, balanced relationship with other people can be met with drawbacks, including self-esteem problems, perfectionist mindset, and low distress tolerance. The interpersonal effectiveness module aims at providing techniques to help manage problems with assertiveness and interpersonal relationships to improve one's sense of self-worth and self-image. This module covers:

- Having other people meet one's objectives through assertion.

- Attaining and maintaining a good relationship.

- Maintaining one's self-respect.

In the interpersonal effectiveness module, individuals are taught skills that maximize their chances of realizing set goals and targets while keeping their level of self-respect intact. Some of the skills patients learn in this module are *DEAR MAN*, *GIVE*, and *FAST*.

- DEAR MAN: This is a skill used to get what one wants from others.

    o **D**escribe: Explain your circumstance using pinpoint facts and figures from a recent happening.

    o **E**xpress: State how you felt about that event and why it is undesirable to you.

    o **A**ssert: Assert yourself by concisely demanding a behavior change.

    o **R**einforce: Reinforce your stance by stating the positive consequences of getting what you want.

    o **M**indful: Be mindful of the present circumstance and put off any distractions or restrictions to stating what you want.

- o **A**ppear: Look self-confident, whether or not you feel so.

- o **N**egotiate: Negotiate when the person is reluctant, and if possible, reach a reasonable compromise.

- GIVE: This skill helps an individual to maintain good relationships with other people, such as family members, friends, and coworkers.

    - o **G**entle: When you engage in a conversation with other people, ensure you use appropriate language. Minimize or avoid sarcasm and never engage in physical confrontations.

    - o **I**nterested: Express interest in whatever the person you are talking to is talking about.

    - o **V**alidate: Show the person you are communicating with that you understand and care about their situation.

    - o **E**asy manner: Ensure that you are always calm and settled in a conversation.

- FAST: This skill, in collaboration with other skills in the interpersonal effectiveness module, helps people maintain their self-respect.

    - o **F**air: Treat yourself and the other individual in a fair manner.

- o **A**pologies: Apologize only once for something you did ineffectively.

- o **S**tick: Stick to your core beliefs and values, and discourage others from taking action against them.

- o **T**ruthful: Avoid lying, as it encourages more lying and harms your self-respect.

Family-Based Treatment (Fbt) For Children And Adolescents

Family-based treatment is another proven aspect of the processes involved in dealing with binge eating disorder. It is as vital for children and adolescents to get the parents involved in the therapeutic process as it is for adult patients. For adults, members of one's current family (marital) or close associates can stand in place of the family of origin for the healing process. The way a patient communicates, relates, or manages disagreements with their family can have a bearing in their recovery process, especially for child and adolescent patients. Through FBT, individuals are made to understand the impact of their eating condition or that of their family member on their family, what factors are supporting the condition, and the line between their family member and the disorder.

The popular notion that one's eating disorder is caused by one's family is not only unhelpful but also untrue. Binge eating disorder is a result of various factors, none of which can induce the disorder on its own. While it is true that the family shapes an individual's background, there is scientific evidence to show that people suffering from eating disorders can originate from disparate backgrounds, may have had different parenting styles, and have different experiences.

Motivation To Change Therapy

Although people with binge eating disorder are fully aware of the negative consequences of their disorder, they are often found to be resistive to therapeutic and recovery processes. They are usually comfortable with the condition, especially in the early phases of treatment, and may not show a lot of interest in getting treated. Due to these impedances to treatment, patients must be motivated to change before the commencement of therapy. To successfully motivate them to change, patients are assigned to categories to enable the therapist to understand them better. These categories are based on the patients' willingness or readiness to change, and include:

- Precontemplation: This category comprises patients who have no will to change, perhaps because they are not aware of the problem they are facing. Here, the patient is made to understand the advantages and disadvantages of their eating disorder.

- Contemplation: Patients at this level have become aware of the problem and are considering changing, but are still not committed to achieving the change. Patients at this stage are encouraged to commit to making a beneficial change to their health.

- Preparation: Patients in this category are willing to do what it takes to change, but are yet to do anything. Patients in this category actively search for and try to contact a therapist. While under therapy, patients are prompted to identify all factors restricting them from taking action and are introduced to valuable skills for solving their eating disorder.

- Action: Patients who are in the phase of altering their behaviors. The treatment plan at this stage is geared toward ensuring a change in patient behavior.

- Maintenance: These patients have already successfully modified their behaviors, and are therefore in the phase of preventing a relapse. At this stage, the patient must make a firm stand on their newly developed set of behaviors. All efforts are focused on helping the patient maintain gained skills and modified behaviors.

Before therapy is begun, the category of the patient to be treated must be ascertained, and treatment plans tailored to suit their current level of change; this makes the treatment process more effective and effects more lasting.

Chapter 12

ESSENTIAL TIPS FOR CURING BINGE-EATING

Binge eating can be a very difficult abnormality to correct, often requiring the intervention of weight loss therapists, nutritionists, and psychologists to treat. However, the most important person in the therapy is the sufferer himself. This is because engaging with these professionals does not guarantee recovery from bingeing habits if the sufferer does not show the same commitment. Only one person is going to be around to deal with the impulses for binge-eating when they arrive. If the sufferer's response does not follow the right reaction pathway, it could lead to results that bring about a complete relapse.

This chapter offers more valuable advice in the form of tips to deal with binge-eating.

Exercise as a palliative measure

I have advised you not to take up dieting or stringent fasting as a medium for losing weight if you are a binge eater. So, you have the right to ask how you can lose weight. Well, the most experienced weight loss experts will tell you that to lose weight, nutrition, and exercise play integral roles. Therefore, the way out is for you to increase the quantity of exercise that you do daily. Pick up aerobic and cardiovascular exercises.

Most experts advise that you get in some exercise, however light early in the morning when you wake up. Regular exercise produces endorphins which are like feel-good hormones that can boost your moods. Find a way to work it into your morning routine. Exercise can give you a turbo lift to start the day and make it less likely that you will experience depressive thoughts that may trigger a binge.

You do not need to hit the gym every day either. Rather, you can also increase the physical activity you take in. For instance, you should take the stairs more frequently than ever before. Shun the elevators for now. When you are not in a hurry, walk a block before you hail a cab. Generally, engage in more physical activity than ever before.

Medications

It is normal for your doctor to prescribe medications to you as part of the treatment for your binge eating disorder. Talk therapy, such as cognitive behavioral therapy and interpersonal therapy, is usually the first line of treatment for people with the bingeing disorder, and research has shown that CBT is a better treatment modality than medications. However, therapists usually prescribe CBT in conjunction with medications for overall wellness. Furthermore, if talk therapy does not produce results or is not an available mode of treatment for a particular patient, then medications alone could be prescribed for treatment. It is possible for bingeing to occur alongside other mental anomalies like depression and anxiety. If you are suffering from any of these conditions, then treating it with medications such as antidepressants can help fight against your bingeing.

One of the most common drugs physicians prescribe for the treatment of binge eating is Lisdexamfetamine dimesylate or Vyvanse. It is approved by the FDA and recommended for treating binge eating in adults. Though studies are still ongoing as to how exactly the drug helps on the treatment of bingeing, clinical trials have shown that it reduces binges. This trials which involved administration of the drug in BED patients produced findings that suggested that patients who took the drug did not show as many bingeing tendencies as those who did not.

Anti-seizure medications have also been used to treat binge eating. Drugs like Topiramate can assist in getting you off bingeing; however, it comes with side effects that may impact your health greatly. Plenty of other drug types, including Dasotraline, certain weight loss drugs, and anti-addiction medications, are under research as possible drugs to treat bingeing. With these drugs and more, you can be sure that in the future, there would be a myriad of chemical options for treating the menace of bingeing.

Antidepressants have also been used to further the treatment of binge eating. These drugs aim to influence the brain chemicals that regulate your mood, and since negative moods have been linked with bingeing behavior, these drugs can help to keep your mood light and keep you away from bingeing.

It is popularly believed among therapists that depression is linked to binge eating. This assertion has led to many scientists purporting that if both abnormalities are linked in some way, then similar therapy pathways can be used to treat them. If that is the case, then similar medications could also work against both conditions. Fluvoxamine and Sertraline are two common antidepressants used to ward off depression by injecting more serotonin, a mood controlling chemical, into the body. These drugs are known as selective serotonin reuptake inhibitors, or SSRIs, and are known to reduce bingeing behaviors. Fluoxetine and Prozac are other SSRIs that might help combat bingeing. Additionally, medications such as Bupropion and tricyclic antidepressants might also help ward off binge eating.

Regular Sleep

If we are throwing a broad net to bring in as many potential aids for defeating BED, then regular sleep is highly recommended as well. Regular sleep reduces anxiety, stress, and promotes better mental health. All these can combine to ensure that the incidence of binge-eating is reduced. Besides that, some sufferers engage in nocturnal binges. For them, being up at night is a trigger for binge-eating. If you experience this, then getting some regular sleep may be a great place to start your therapy from.

Avoiding Temptations

When the eyes do not see, the mind does not grieve. This is also particularly true when it comes to binge-eating. You are not really going to get rid of processed foods, for instance, if your kitchen is filled up with them. Cutting your excessive chocolate addiction is not going to work if you still keep large slabs of chocolate in your refrigerator. You are less likely to quit alcoholism if your minibar is stocked with dozens of your favorite brands of beer. Getting rid of temptations is a first call to defeating overeating. Try to empty out the foods we have deemed unhealthy from your most immediate surroundings. The sight of a packet of something forbidden for you to eat can severely test your resolve. So, do not set yourself up to be tested. Instead, keep the things you would rather not eat far away from you. It could make all the difference.

Build a Support Network

Addictions are often hard to fight alone. They can be demanding, tasking, and break your motivation numerous times. You brighten your chances of defeating the addiction if you involve some of your closest relatives and friends in the battle. They can help you monitor your diet, offer timely advice, and oversee your recovery process. You have nothing to lose by involving one or two people close to you and enlisting them as support against food addiction.

How to Manage a Binge Eater

Binge-eating can be a frustrating disorder for an individual to deal with. If your child, friend, companion, or associate is caught up in binge eating, you would want to do everything you can to assist them in combating it. The following tips are meant for people who want to render assistance or are primary caregivers for a binge-eater, especially parents of a binge-eater.

- Don't get into the blame game: It is important to understand that the bingeing is not exclusively a fault of the victim. You must show understanding and empathy, and try to help the victim as well as you can.

- Be objective: Sometimes, it is difficult to figure out why the victim binges. It is normal to feel angry and frustrated at not being able to control the situation. You must understand that the person suffering from the anomaly already feels bad or ashamed about themselves and their behavior. Do not worsen the situation; instead, try to remain open-minded.

- If it is your child who is trying to recover from binge eating, chances are you would accompany them to see a therapist. You could become an active person in the treatment process by being more involved. Ask the therapist how the therapy is going, and ensure the patient sticks to the treatment plan. Being actively involved in the treatment process ensure better involvement of the patient.

- Keep only healthy foods in the house and encourage the patient to eat regularly and well.

- Ensure you are a good example for the person you are trying to support. If you are asking them to eat healthy foods regularly, make sure you are doing the same. Be a good role model for them. Also, do not make comparisons that involve their physique or weight as a joke or otherwise.

- Do not grow impatient and give up. Bingeing is not an easy behavior to give up. Even when the binge eater does things that are unhelpful to their condition, don't get angry and leave them to their own devices. Offer to help them all the time.

- You could also use the support of a Support group. If you are a parent to a binge eater, join a parent's support group to learn about dealing with children suffering from binge-eating disorder from people who probably have more experience in the matter.

Prevention of a Relapse

It can be very difficult to rid oneself of binge-eating completely. It is normal to see people slip up and revert to their old bingeing ways while in therapy. Relapse is a situation where a sufferer in treatment for binge-eating disorder returns to their former state of negativity and false assessments about their weight, body, and food. Relapse usually occurs when you respond impulsively to the factors that trigger your bingeing. It is therefore important to know these triggers and know how to handle them appropriately so that you would not binge impulsively. The following tips would help you combat the obstacles standing in the way of your recovery and prevent a relapse.

- Develop a support network: During recovery, ensure to always be in the company of people, such as family members, friends, or associates, who genuinely love and care about you. Make sure they are aware of your condition, and that they are on hand to render their support in difficult times. Although it is usually hard to reach out for help, you need to understand that having people around can go a long way towards keeping you on track and helping you avoid a relapse. If you don't feel very comfortable being around people, make a list of 'emergency contacts' to reach out to when you notice that you are slipping back to your old ways.

- Cut out negativity: Avoid surrounding yourself with things or people who might influence you to take drastic and impulse actions on your body – for example, a person who constantly draws comparisons between their perfect body and your "not-so-perfect" physique. You must also distance yourself from negative thoughts, as they can trigger you to slip up and take unhelpful actions.

- Know your triggers: Though everyone has their own triggers, depression, anxiety, and loneliness are common to most binge eaters. A trigger can also come in the form of an event or a holiday. Having lots of food lying around during festive seasons, ceremonies, or any time at all can also constitute a trigger.

- Write out your trigger management plan: After identifying your triggers, detail out a plan that can help you manage every trigger. Know when the triggers could surface, and the appropriate action to take once you feel them. You may talk to a friend, take a walk, or write in your diary when a trigger shows up.

- Eat well and regularly: Unlike drugs and smoking, you cannot completely stay off food. You must eat. If you stay off food for a long time or deprive yourself of it intentionally, you are bound to overeat eventually. Make an eating plan and stay true to it.

- Do not be too critical of yourself: If in the process of receiving the treatment, you slip up and eat a snack or meal when you were not supposed to eat, do not lose hope. Don't throw in the towel and lose faith in the treatment process because of a slip-up. Forgive yourself quickly and move on with the treatment plan.

- Celebrate victories: You need to cheer yourself on. Consider things like sticking to your meal plan, successfully managing a trigger, and fighting back negative thoughts as victories in your fight against bingeing. Take time to celebrate every victory, as it motivates you to carry on.

Vital Tips for Curing Binge Eating

Binge eating can eat into your self-esteem and sense of self-worth quickly. These simple tips below should help set you on track to getting your normal life back.

- Avoid dieting: It has proven beyond reasonable doubt now that dieting does not work for a binge-eater. Any weight lost through dieting would eventually be regained through excessive or binge eating in the following weeks, months, or years. Restrictive diets are strongly linked to binge-eating. Rather than cutting a whole chunk of food off your daily diet, focus on eating more balanced, healthier foods as they improve overall health, and prevent bingeing.

- Don't skip meals: Skipping meals can induce abnormal craving, which can lead to bingeing behavior.

- Mindfulness helps: Mindfulness is a technique that teaches one to pay attention to the present moment, rather than being lost in the past or wandering too deep into the future. By practicing mindfulness, you can ascertain when you are full and no longer hungry, and hence, no longer need to eat. You can get rid of binge eating this way.

- Drink lots of water: Water is a low-calorie alternative to most foods. Staying adequately hydrated throughout the day ensures you do not develop wild cravings or eat excessively.

- Practice yoga: Yoga combines various exercises with certain poses and meditations to provide stress and depression relief. As stress and depression are heavily linked to binge eating, doubt yoga is a good fit for stopping or alleviating bingeing thoughts and behaviors.

- Up your nutrition game: Eat foods that are sure to keep you feeling fuller for longer. A good example of such foods is fiber. The digestive tract digests fiber slowly, therefore eating fiber ensures you feel hungry less often, and reduces your tendencies to binge-eat.

- Clear out: Junk foods are the usual suspects when it comes to the foods binge water are most drawn to while bingeing. Do a massive clear out of your kitchen and refrigerator on junk foods, and replace them with better options, such as fiber and whole grains.

These tips are by no means exhaustive, but they are a good place for you to start the fight against binge-eating. I wish you the very best of luck.

Conclusion

The binge-eating disorder often goes undetected in most people who suffer from it. They simply think their overeating is normal. Most sufferers fail to realize that the collection of symptoms, such as guilt after eating, actually signal something deeper. So, they overeat, get to feel guilty and then overeat again to cover their shame. This does not have to be your relationship with food.

Granted, most people do not even understand the relationship between them and the way they eat. They simply eat when they feel hungry. They also eat when they are stressed. They put something in their mouth when they are happy. And then, eat off their anxiety and fears too. The point I am making is that most emotional overeaters are not even aware of the condition. Luckily, having gone through this book, you now have the knowledge you need to defeat BED as a sufferer or a therapist.

BED depends on certain triggers that often precipitate an urge to overeat. While some of the factors are inborn or beyond your control, it is certainly possible to limit their potential effects. The central theme of binge-eating disorder is a loss of control over the triggers for eating. It is a confirmation of the loss of rational control of eating. Therefore, the first step in getting rid of binge-eating is to acknowledge its presence and cause. Thereafter, you can proceed to chip it off one episode at a time. Keeping a food diary, watching what you eat, and cutting out sugar and processed foods are first-line treatment options for binge-eating disorder. These should be coupled with cognitive behavioral therapy at the very least, to restore some self-esteem.

Above all, you must always remember that eating is a process that is meant to be triggered by actual hunger. Eating can never be an effective weapon to combat your emotions. Hiding beyond your plates when your emotions are haywire is only going to put you under even more unneeded emotional stress. Understand that food is meant to fill your belly, and not cloud the mind. It is a response to hunger pangs and not emotional pangs. Food has never been a solution for anything aside, hunger. Do not make it one now.

Beating binge-eating disorder is possible if you offer the right commitment to the process, as outlined in this book. As I mentioned before, though, you need to actually put all the info in this book to practice if you are to see positive changes almost immediately. The ball is firmly in your court now. You can choose to dither and allow food to continue to run your emotions. Or you can strike now and get binge-eating out of your routine. Your mind and brain were built to hold and process thoughts, your stomach to deal with food. Do not switch the roles and put your stomach in charge of your thoughts. Instead, strive to get rid of emotional eating. Stamp out binge-eating NOW!!!

Good luck!.

Printed in the USA
CPSIA information can be obtained
at www.ICGtesting.com
LVHW020829191024
794260LV00011B/477